PAINT AND WALLPAPER

HOME REPAIR
AND IMPROVEMENT

PAINT AND WALLPAPER

BY THE EDITORS OF
TIME-LIFE BOOKS

TIME-LIFE BOOKS, NEW YORK

TIME-LIFE BOOKS

Founder: Henry R. Luce 1898-1967

Editor-in-Chief: Hedley Donovan
Chairman of the Board: Andrew Heiskell
President: James R. Shepley

Vice Chairman: Roy E. Larsen

Managing Editor: Jerry Korn
Assistant Managing Editors: Ezra Bowen, David Maness, Martin Mann
Planning Director: Oliver E. Allen
Art Director: Sheldon Cotler
Chief of Research: Beatrice T. Dobie
Director of Photography: Melvin L. Scott
Senior Text Editors: Diana Hirsh, William Frankel
Assistant Planning Director: Carlotta Kerwin
Assistant Art Director: Arnold C. Holeywell
Assistant Chief of Research: Myra Mangan

Publisher: Joan D. Manley
Associate Publisher: John D. McSweeney
General Manager: John Steven Maxwell
Assistant Publisher, North America: Carl G. Jaeger
Assistant Publisher, International: David J. Walsh
Business Manager: Peter B. Barnes
Promotion Director: Paul R. Stewart
Mail Order Sales Director: John L. Canova
Public Relations Director: Nicholas Benton

HOME REPAIR AND IMPROVEMENT

Editorial Staff for Paint and Wallpaper:

Editor: John Paul Porter
Assistant Editor: David L. Harrison
Picture Editor: Rhea Finkelstein
Designer: Herbert H. Quarmby
Associate Designer: Robert McKee
Text Editors: Marion Buhagiar, Robert L. Tschirky
Staff Writers: Valentin Chu, Simone D. Gossner, Lee Hassig, Ruth Kelton, Don Nelson, Isabelle Rubin, Sandra Streepey
Researcher: Joan McCullough
Art Associates: Faye Eng, Kaye Sherry Hirsh, Richard Salcer
Editorial Assistant: Eleanor G. Kask

Editorial Production
Production Editor: Douglas B. Graham
Assistant Production Editors: Gennaro C. Esposito, Feliciano Madrid
Quality Director: Robert L. Young
Assistant Quality Director: James J. Cox
Associate: Serafino J. Cambareri
Copy Staff: Eleanore W. Karsten (chief), Ricki Tarlow, Florence Keith, Pearl Sverdlin
Picture Department: Dolores A. Littles, Barbara S. Simon
Traffic: Carmen McLellan

THE CONSULTANTS: Deanne Raffel, the general consultant for this book, studied industrial design at The Pratt Institute in Manhattan and has taught courses in home repair at The New School in New York City and in the Adult Education Division of the Great Neck, N.Y. public school system.

Harris Mitchell, special consultant for Canada, has been working in the field of home repair and improvement for more than two decades. His experience ranges from editing *Canadian Homes* magazine to writing a syndicated newspaper column, "You Wanted to Know," and he is the editor or author of a number of books on home improvement.

Valuable assistance was given by the following departments and individuals of Time Inc.: Editorial Production, Norman Airey; Photographic Laboratory, George Karas.

Contents

Painting Like a Pro

M marks the spot. A roller thickly loaded with fresh paint letters a large ''M'' as the first step in painting a wall. The letter lies within a 3-foot square, the first section to be covered; the section is then filled in crisscross strokes across and around the M. Then an adjoining section is painted the same way with a fresh load of paint.

Almost everyone has painted at least a room in his home—and finished the job a bit dissatisfied, convinced there must be ways to make the work go faster and easier while simultaneously producing a better result. There are such ways. Every trade has its tricks, and painting is no exception. If you know them, you will be able to save yourself time and effort and do the job right.

A painter's craft is not merely a matter of procedures and techniques. It begins with an understanding of what paint is and how it works. The coating that you put on your house creates a tough film that 1) bonds itself to either a fresh, new surface or an old, uneven one; 2) covers and helps to protect that surface against the assaults of weather, airborne chemicals and dirt; and 3) remains flexible enough to stay intact for years while the walls settle, vibrate, and expand and contract with changes in temperature. The coating that accomplishes all of this is only about five thousandths of an inch thick —just a little thicker than a page of this book.

Almost any liquid that dries into such a coat for a surface can be considered a paint and an astonishing variety of materials have gone into these mixtures. In India, boiled rice was used to bind paint together; milk and lime have been principal ingredients in popular coatings; and there are some modern paints that consist essentially of colored cement or dissolved rubber. But most of the paints in common use contain certain types of ingredients, each with a specific function. Substances called pigments, made from minute particles of earth, metals or chemical compounds, give paint its color (varnishes, being colorless, are unpigmented paint). The ability to form a thin, tough film comes from ingredients called resins, often known as binders. These resins were originally the natural secretions of certain plants and insects, but now consist mostly of man-made chemicals—plastics—such as alkyds, acrylics, polyvinyls or urethanes. Chemical agents called plasticizers keep the paint elastic after it dries. And to make the mixture of pigment, resin and plasticizer thin enough to be used with a brush or roller, it is combined with a solvent that may be water, a mineral spirit such as benzine or a plant derivative such as turpentine.

No one paint is right for every surface—and no paint of any kind will work well if you use the wrong tools to prepare the surface or apply the paint. The chart on pages 8 and 9 matches both interior and exterior paints to almost any surface that you are likely to encounter; on pages 18-19 and 54-55 you will find pictures and descriptions of all the tools you will need for any painting job. The remainder of this chapter deals with the specific problems and the techniques of interior painting.

A Coating for Every Surface

There is a paint for every wall, but there is no single coating that can be used in every circumstance. Some finishes will not adhere to certain surfaces. No interior paint, for example, will last long on an exterior wall, because it cracks under the expansion and contraction caused by temperature changes. Oil paints wrinkle and peel if they are applied to fresh plaster; as the plaster dries, the moisture and alkali it releases deform the film of paint. A finish such as varnish, which forms an impervious seal against water, soon blisters on a moist wall.

The wrong coating can actually damage a wall surface. Latex paint, which is thinned with water, promotes rust if it is applied directly to iron or steel. The thinners in other paints can dissolve glue; if paint containing such a solvent is used over wallpaper, both paper and paint could peel right off the wall.

To help you avoid such costly errors, the chart on these pages identifies finishing materials suitable for the common surfaces. The vertical columns at the left and right of the chart list the kinds of surfaces to be covered in four sections: raw wood, raw masonry, bare metal and previously finished surfaces. Major types of interior and exterior coatings are listed across the top. Suppose you want to paint a new plaster wall. Read down the left column under raw masonry to "plaster," then follow the horizontal row of boxes to the right. You will find dots or footnote numbers in the boxes beneath glossy and flat latex paint, rubber-base paint and alkyd primer, and beneath a whole sequence of other coatings. To learn more about these finishes—what they are made of, whether or not they are toxic, how fast they dry, if they are odor-free, what kind of painting tool to apply them with—turn to pages 16-19 for interior coatings, or pages 52-53 for exterior materials.

1 These coatings are available in different compositions for exterior and interior painting; use the type appropriate to the job.
2 Sand glossy finishes before painting over them.
3 Use the type formulated for masonry.
4 Use the epoxy-paint type.
5 Use the type formulated for metal.
6 Use the type formulated for galvanized metal.

Surfaces	Glossy Oil Paint (1)	Glossy Alkyd Paint (1)	Glossy Latex Paint (1)	Flat Oil Paint (1)	Flat Alkyd Paint (1)	Flat Latex Paint (1)	Latex Shingle Paint (1)	Oil or Alkyd Paint (1)	Rubber-Base Shingle Paint	Cement-Base Paint (1)	Epoxy Paint (1)	Urethane Paint (1)	Porch and Floor Paint (1)	Marine Paint (1)	Multicolor Paint
Raw Wood															
Wood, plywood or clapboard	●	●		●	●						●	●	●	●	
Particle board	●	●		●	●						●		●		
Hardboard	●	●	●	●	●	●					●	●	●	●	
Rough wood siding				●	●	●	●	●							
Wood shakes and shingles				●	●	●	●	●							
Exterior wood trim	●	●	●									●		●	
Raw Masonry															
Plaster			●			●				●					●
Gypsum wallboard			●			●									●
Concrete			●			●			●	●	3	3	3		●
Cinder block			●			●			●	●			3		●
Brick			●		●	●			●	●	3		3		●
Stucco			●	3	●					●					●
Asbestos-cement shingles or board					●	●	●	3							
Ceramic tile or glass											●	●		4	
Bare Metal															
Steel or iron	5	5									●				
Galvanized metal															
Aluminum	5	5	5	5	5	5					●	●			
Copper or bronze											●	●			
Previous Surface Covering															
Wallpaper			●		●	●									●
Flat oil paint or primer	●	●		●	●			●					●		
Flat alkyd paint or primer	●	●		●	●			●				●	●		
Flat latex paint or primer	●	●	●	●	●	●	●		●	●		●			●
Glossy oil paint (2)	●	●		●	●							●	●		
Alkyd glossy paint or varnish (2)	●	●		●	●							●	●		
Glossy latex paint (2)	●	●	●	●	●	●						●			●
Epoxy paint or varnish (2)	●	●		●	●						●		4	4	
Polyurethane paint or varnish (2)	●	●		●	●							●	●		
Rubber-base paint		●	●	●	●					●			●		
Cement paint										●					
Zinc-dust primer	6	6													
Zinc-rich metal primers	●	●	●	●	●							●	●		
Aluminum paint	●	●	●	●	●			●				●	●		
Block filler		3	●	3	3	●	●		●	●	3	●	3		●
Wood filler	●	●						●							
Paintable wood sealer	●	●		●	●	●		●				●			
Paintable masonry sealer				3	●			●	●			3			●
Bleach	●	●		●	●		●	●			●	●	●		

8

Paint/surface compatibility chart.

Surfaces \ Coatings	Latex Sand Paint	Latex Texture Paint	Dripless Paint	Fire-Retardant Paint	Alkyd Varnish	Polyurethane Varnish (1)	Epoxy Varnish	Moisture-Cured Urethane Varnish (1)	Spar Varnish	Acrylic Lacquer	Shellac	Oil Stain	Water Stain	Alcohol Stain	Exterior Latex Stain	Varnish Stain	Bleach	Oil Primer (1)	Alkyd Primer (1)	Latex Primer (1)	Oil-Cement Primer (1)	Zinc-Rich Metal Primer	Zinc-Dust Primer	Aluminum Paint	Wood Sealer	Masonry Sealer	Silicone Water Repellent	Block Filler	Wood Filler	Paintable Wood Preservative	Creosote
Raw Wood																															
Wood, plywood or clapboard			●		●	●	●	●	●		●	●	●	●	●	●	●	●	●					●	●				●	●	●
Particle board			●		●	●		●	●		●	●	●	●	●	●		●	●					●	●		●				
Hardboard	●	●	●	●	●	●	●	●	●		●							●	●	●				●	●						
Rough wood siding												●		●	●		●	●	●					●		●				●	●
Wood shakes and shingles												●		●	●		●	●	●					●		●				●	●
Exterior wood trim					●	●	●	●	●			●			●	●		●	●					●	●					●	●
Raw Masonry																															
Plaster	●	●		●						●								3	●							●					
Gypsum wallboard	●	●		●						●									●												
Concrete	●	●		●														3	●							●	●				
Cinder block	●	●		●														3	●							●	●				
Brick	●	●		●		●	●			●								●	●							●	●				
Stucco	●	●		●														3	●							●	●				
Asbestos-cement shingles or board	●	●		●																											
Ceramic tile or glass							●	●																							
Bare Metal																															
Steel or iron							●			●								5	5	5		●	●	●							
Galvanized metal																		6	6	6		●	●	●							
Aluminum						●	●			●								5	5	5		●		●							
Copper or bronze						●	●			●								5				●									
Previous Surface Covering																															
Wallpaper																		●	●												
Flat oil paint or primer			●	●	●	●																		●							
Flat alkyd paint or primer			●	●	●	●																		●							
Flat latex paint or primer	●	●	●	●	●	●																		●							
Glossy oil paint (2)			●	●	●																			●							
Alkyd glossy paint or varnish (2)			●	●	●			●																●							
Glossy latex paint (2)	●	●	●	●																				●							
Epoxy paint or varnish (2)							●																								
Polyurethane paint or varnish (2)						●		●																							
Rubber-base paint			●																												
Cement paint																															
Zinc-dust primer																							●								
Zinc-rich metal primers																						●	●	●							
Aluminum paint			●	●																				●							
Block filler	●	●		●															●							●					
Wood filler			●		●	●	●		●		●	●	●	●		●		●	●										●		
Paintable wood sealer			●		●	●			●		●	●	●	●		●		●	●								●				
Paintable masonry sealer	●	●		●																						●					
Bleach			●	●	●	●	●		●		●	●	●	●	●	●		●						●			●			●	

9

Getting at the High Places:
How to Choose and Use a Ladder

Two types of ladders are used around the home: stepladders for reaching to standard ceiling height and extension ladders for higher elevations. Most people feel secure enough on a stepladder; it rests steadily on four legs and is not very tall. Climbing a narrow, springy, extension ladder, on the other hand, often presents a new and perhaps uneasy prospect. Before investing in an extension ladder, rent one or borrow a neighbor's to try it out.

Ladders are made of wood, aluminum, magnesium or fiberglass. For most homeowners, aluminum ladders are the best. They are no more expensive than wooden ones, weigh about 20 per cent less, are easy to maintain and durable. Ladders are classified as Type I, Type II or Type III, depending on how strong they are. A Type I ladder, the strongest, is the best choice. A so-called industrial model, it is rated for loads up to 250 pounds, but can support four times that, and although heavier than ladders of less capacity, it is not much more expensive. For added assurance, look for a "UL" seal, which means the ladder has been approved by the independent testing agency, Underwriters' Laboratory.

Ladders by themselves may be insufficient for certain jobs. Stairwells with high ceilings, for example, may be impossible to paint or paper without a platform like the one shown overleaf. Exterior painting, particularly with a spray gun (pages 74 and 75), is facilitated by using brackets called ladder jacks to support a platform of planks from two extension ladders. No ladder is satisfactory where the ground is uneven or where the structure of the house prevents setting up the ladder within reach of the work. The only safe access in such cases is scaffolding erected by a professional.

Even the best ladders are dangerous. Protect yourself by respecting a few simple safety rules. If the ladder is new, borrowed, rented or put to use after a long period of storage, inspect it for cracks, splits, twisted or jammed parts, and loose screws, rivets or rungs. If the ladder is seriously defective, do not try to repair it; get a new one.

Always face a ladder when you climb and descend it, and use both hands to hold onto the rungs. It is not a good idea to carry tools in your hands or pockets while climbing. Set them on the shelf of a stepladder; if you are working on an extension ladder, place them in a bucket and hoist them up with a rope. If you must work high on an extension ladder, have someone hold the rails. For added security, use a ladder stabilizer (overleaf), an accessory that not only steadies the ladder but makes it easier to use near windows. But do not, in any case, work too high: never stand above the third highest rung or step of a ladder.

Never forget your balance. Overreaching to one side leads to the most serious falls. A traditional rule for avoiding it is: keep your belt buckle within the space bounded by the ladder's side rails. Do not carry a paint bucket with one hand while you are painting. Instead, place it on the bucket shelf of a stepladder or hang it from a rung of an extension ladder with an S hook (opposite).

The proper care and storage of your ladder will keep it safer. Protect a wooden ladder with clear wood preservative, spar varnish or shellac. Hang any ladder on at least three large, strong hooks in a dry place, far from heating pipes or a stove. Periodically, inspect the hoisting rope, tighten all fixed parts and lubricate all movable parts.

Some Ladder "Don'ts"

Don't set up a ladder in front of a closed, unlocked door; either lock the door or open it.
Don't use an unstable object—a rock or a brick—to level the ladder's feet.
Don't use a ladder in a high wind.
Don't stand a ladder on ice or snow.
Don't lean the top of a ladder against a windowpane or screen.
Don't link ladders to add height.
Don't place a metal ladder near electric wires.
Don't step between ladders.
Don't paint a wooden ladder. Paint hides new cracks and splits.

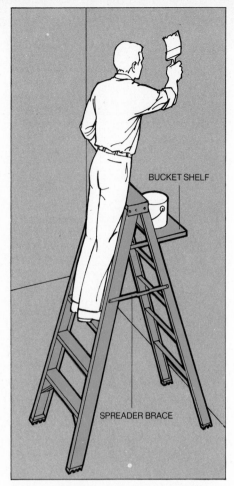

Using a stepladder. Always open a stepladder to its fullest extent, lock its spreader braces into place and push the bucket shelf down as far as it will go. Place the four legs on level ground or a level floor; if the floor is slippery and the ladder is not fitted with rubber shoes, set it on a piece of old rug or a rubber mat. Climb the ladder one step at a time, always holding to upper steps with both hands as you climb; do not hold onto the side rails while climbing. Never stand or sit on top of the ladder, on the step immediately below the top or on the bucket shelf (the drawing above shows the highest safe working position).

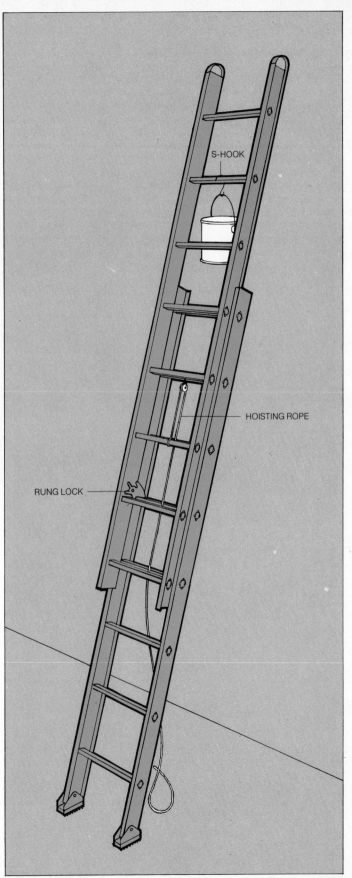

S-HOOK

HOISTING ROPE

RUNG LOCK

Setting up an extension ladder. Place the ladder flat on the ground, with its bottom a few inches from the vertical surface to be painted and the movable extension section facing down. Raise the top end. Then, grasping the rungs hand over hand "walk" the ladder to a vertical position *(above)*. Now lift the bottom slightly and shift the ladder outward so it leans firmly against the wall.

Using an extension ladder. Adjust the angle of the ladder so that when the ladder is extended the distance from its top to the ground will be about four times the distance between its bottom and the wall. A ladder set closer to the wall may tip over; one set farther away may sag or break under the weight of the climber. Be sure the feet are level. Dig away a high spot or use a wide plank or cement block to compensate for uneven ground. Or, bolt an accessory called a ladder leveler to a side rail to extend one of the feet.

To extend the ladder, pull the loose end of the hoisting rope until the upper section reaches the desired height, then fasten the sections with the rung lock. (Caution: the upper section should overlap the lower by at least 3 feet.) While you are aloft, keep one hand on a rung; if you must free both hands briefly, move one leg between two rungs and hook a foot around a side rail.

Advantages of a stabilizer. A ladder stabilizer provides a broad base for the top of an extension ladder so that it is less likely to twist away from a wall. Stabilizers come in a variety of materials and designs. The one shown at right is made of square aluminum tubing bent into a shallow U that is wide enough to serve as a bridge across a single window, and lifts the ladder away from the wall for easier access to roof overhangs. The stabilizer is fastened to the rails of the ladder with clamps; they are tightened by wing nuts and are installed so that the top rung supports the stabilizer. Nonskid pads on the stabilizer prevent the ladder from slipping or marring the wall.

Another accessory called a ladder hook fastens a ladder by its top two rungs to the roof peak. The rungs lie on the shingles for secure footing.

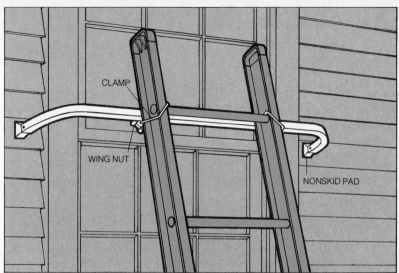

A platform for a stairwell. To paint the ceiling and upper walls above a staircase, use a simple platform: a straight ladder, a stepladder and a 2-by-10-inch plank. (Use a ''scaffold grade'' plank, an especially strong type of lumber. If the plank spans more than 6 feet, set a second plank on top of it to give it added strength.) Assemble the platform by leaning the straight ladder against the wall. Unless the upper ends of the ladder are fitted with rubber tips, protect the wall from scratches by wrapping the ends of the ladder with rags. Set the stepladder at the top of the stairs and lay the plank on a lower rung of the stepladder and on whichever rung of the straight ladder makes the plank level. Paint as much of the wall around the ladder as you can, then disassemble the platform and finish the wall by standing at the stair railing and leaning over it.

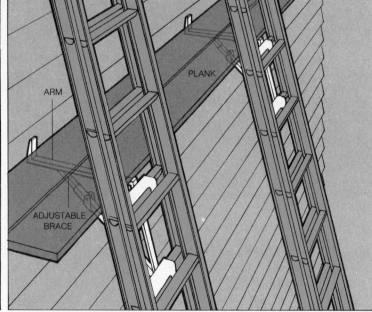

Turning ladders into scaffolding. Two sound, Type I extension ladders, two 2-by-10-inch scaffold-grade planks 10 feet long, and a pair of ladder jacks like those shown above are the ingredients for this one-man painting scaffold. To erect the platform, adjust the lengths of the ladders so that the rung at the height you wish to stand—no more than 20 feet—will lie about 2½ feet from the wall (3½ feet for spraying).

Lean the ladders against the wall no more than 6 feet apart and attach the ladder jacks. The lightweight, aluminum ones shown here clip onto the rungs; other models are designed to be fastened to the ladder rails. Level the arm of each jack by adjusting its brace. Then, with a helper, carry the planks one at a time up the ladder and lay them, side by side, across the arms of the ladder jacks. Be careful when working from this kind of platform; there are no handholds or safety rails to keep you from falling if you lose your balance.

Doing the Right Things in the Right Order

Whether you paint a single room or the interior of an entire house, you will achieve the best results with the least fuss if you take the time to plan your work. Doing the right things in the right order is the first essential. To begin with, you need to know how much paint to buy and how long the job is likely to take; these questions can be answered with the rules of thumb in the box below.

Next comes the choice of paint from among the dozens available. The chart on pages 8 and 9 lists the full range of interior and exterior paints; on pages 14-17, the advantages and disadvantages of interior coatings in the chart are described in detail.

From this point on the work falls into three stages: the preparation of surfaces, the painting itself and the final cleanup. Pages 20-31 discuss the preparation and, where necessary, the repair of plaster, wallboard, wood and wallpaper. Pages 32-43 deal with paint mixing, rollerwork and brushwork, and also the correct sequence for painting a room. And pages 44 and 45 cover the final stage, in which a room is returned to its original condition and the tools are cleaned and stored.

The most important part of a home-painting plan concerns the painter personally. If you have not painted for some time, you may become painfully aware of muscles you did not know you had. Painting probably requires more lifting, stretching and bending than most daily tasks. Plan the job to take into account your own capacities. If you schedule your work sensibly and allow for coffee breaks and lunch, you will finish in good condition, right through to the cleanup stage, and enjoy the results all the more.

How Much Paint? How Much Time?

The worst place to estimate how much paint you need for a job is at the paint store. Figure out the area you have to cover at home.

For a rectangular room with average-sized windows and doors *(below),* first measure the length and width, round off each figure to the nearest foot, and add them together. Multiply that total by the room height and then double that result. The final figure is the area of your wall in square feet. From this total, subtract about 15 square feet for each of the windows and 21 square feet

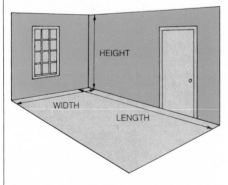

for each door. Ceiling area is the length times the width of the room.

If the room is an unusual shape, measure the height and width of each rectangular section to be painted. Multiply these figures to get the area, then add them together for the total area needing paint.

A stairwell often forms a triangular shape. For the area of the triangle, multiply the lengths of the horizontal and vertical legs and divide by two.

If you plan to paint the trim with a different-colored paint, figure these areas separately. Allow about 21 square feet for each side of a door and 15 square feet for the trim on an average window. A baseboard area is the product of its height times its total length, which is generally the same as the perimeter of the room.

When you know the total area you will cover, you have half the information you need to order paint. The rest depends on the covering capacity of your paint and the surface it must coat. If your walls are smooth, figure on covering 400 feet with a gallon of finishing paint. Divide your area figure by that amount to arrive at the number of gallons you need for a first coat. If you are using finishing paint on porous, rough or previously unpainted walls, the gallon will cover about 350 feet. You can count on more coverage for the second coat—about 450 feet per gallon for a smooth-surfaced wall and 400 feet per gallon for a rough wall.

One gallon of paint is generally ample for a 12-by-15-foot room with an 8-foot ceiling and smooth, previously painted walls; the ceiling of the same room would take 1½ quarts (if you must buy 2 quarts you can reserve the extra for repairs). Professional painters often

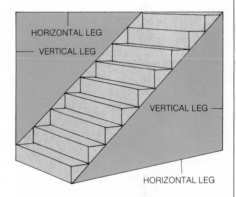

allow for about one quarter as much trim paint as wall paint, but you can make a more accurate and economical purchase if you calculate the trim area as suggested above.

Estimating time brings in a new set of variables. You are likely to cover about 120 square feet of an ordinary surface in an hour, or about 100 square feet of bare wood or plaster. Thus, you will probably be able to paint that 12-by-15 room with one coat in four to five hours —if you do not have much patching to do. Extensive repairs can more than double your working time. And if you apply two coats, you must allow time for the first coat to dry—a matter of two to 36 hours (check the label of your paint can). On a major job, however, the variables tend to cancel each other out. For example, you can safely figure on five or six days to paint seven rooms, including preparation and cleanup.

A Guide to Interior Coatings

The chart on pages 8 and 9 can serve as a ready reference for matching interior and exterior coatings to almost every surface. Here and on the pages that follow, the interior coatings listed in the chart are discussed in detail.

In this guide, 20 types of interior coatings are grouped in four categories. First come general-purpose finishing paints for walls and ceilings—often the only paints you will need, especially if surfaces are in good condition. Next is a small group of special-purpose finishes that conceal uneven or damaged walls, or have other unique properties (one of these paints will not drip, another slows the spread of fire). The third category includes coatings that enhance the grains and colors of wood. The fourth is devoted to the undercoatings sometimes applied as a base for a finishing coat.

Finishing Paints

Color and gloss are usually the important factors in choosing a finishing paint. While color is a matter of personal preference, gloss affects both appearance and resistance to wear. The three major types of finishing coats—latex, alkyd and oil paints—come in versions labeled flat, semigloss and high gloss by manufacturers. As noted, however, high-gloss latex is somewhat less glossy than comparable versions of the other types.

High-gloss paints are the most wear and moisture resistant because of their relatively high proportion of resin, the ingredient that solidifies into the coating film as the solvent evaporates. The more resin, the heavier—and tougher—the film. The high-resin film of the glossy paints makes them ideal for areas subject to heavy use or frequent washing—particularly kitchens and bathrooms. Semigloss paints afford moderate durability with a less obtrusive shine for most woodwork. Flat paints provide a desirable low-glare surface for walls and ceilings that do not need frequent washing.

Along with latex, oil and alkyd paints, the most commonly used finishes include paints especially suitable for specific surfaces: rubber-base and cement paints for masonry, and epoxy and urethane paints for surfaces that require the toughest and most moistureproof coating available.

Latex Paint
SIMPLIFIES CLEANUP
ODOR FREE
QUICK DRYING

Water is the solvent for latex paint, which is made of plastic resins—either acrylics or tougher polyvinyls. Its water solvent gives latex advantages that have made it the most widely used paint for walls and ceilings. Tools, spills and hands can be cleaned with soap and water while the latex is wet. Latex paint is almost free of odor and harmful fumes, and a coat is usually dry in little more than an hour.

Latex adheres well to most surfaces painted with flat oil or latex paint; it does not adhere to some alkyds, and tends to peel away from any high-gloss finish. Latex can be used over unprimed wallboard, bare masonry and fresh plaster patches that have set but are not quite dry; before applying it to new concrete, wash the surface with a 10 per cent muriatic acid solution, then rinse it clean. Use caution with muriatic acid; wear goggles and rubber gloves.

The water solvent imposes certain limitations on latex paint. Although it can be applied directly over wallpaper, the water in the paint may soak the paper away from the wall. If latex is applied to raw wood the water swells the fibers, roughening the surface—a disadvantage where a smooth finish is desirable. Used on bare steel, it rusts the metal.

Flat latex is less resistant to abrasion and washing than either oil or alkyd paint, and so-called high-gloss latex is less shiny—and less durable—than comparable alkyds or oils. Any paint can be applied over latex.

Alkyd Paint
DURABLE
NEARLY ODORLESS

Any painted or wallpapered surface—or bare wood—can be covered with paint made from a synthetic resin called alkyd (often combined with other resins). This type of paint will not adhere to bare masonry or plaster, and should not be used on bare wallboard because it will raise a nap on the wallboard's paper covering.

Alkyd is the most durable of the common finishing paints. It is also practically odor free. To take advantage of this characteristic, use low-odor solvents (usually listed on the manufacturer's label) for thinning and cleanup—but bear in mind that the fumes of these solvents, though nearly imperceptible, are flammable and toxic. Most alkyds are dry enough for a second coat in four to six hours.

Although some latex paints will not bond well to alkyd, most other paints can be applied over it.

Oil Paint
STRONG SMELLING

For many years paints based on natural plant oils, such as tung or linseed oils, dominated interior painting. An oil paint adheres well to bare wood and to surfaces previously painted with latex, alkyd or oil. In high-gloss and semigloss finishes, it stands up to repeated washing.

Oil paint has so many drawbacks, however, that it has largely been replaced by latex and alkyd mixtures and is now hard to find. In flat finishes, oil paint is less durable than alkyd. It does not adhere to wallpaper, bare wallboard or masonry. The oils in the paint give it a strong, unpleasant odor, and it must be thinned with strong-smelling turpentine or mineral spirits (tools and spills, however, can be cleaned with the relatively odor-free solvents used for alkyd paints). An oil-base paint takes from 12 to 24 hours to dry sufficiently for a second coat, and from two to four days to dry thoroughly.

Although latex will not adhere well to a high-gloss oil paint, alkyds and other oil-base paints can be applied over it.

Rubber-Base Paint
GOOD FOR MASONRY
MOISTUREPROOF
VERY FAST DRYING

This moisture-resistant coating, a liquefied rubber, can be applied directly to bare masonry; bare brick, however, must first be sealed with a clear varnish, and new concrete should be washed with a 10 per cent muriatic acid solution, then rinsed clean. (As always, when preparing masonry with muriatic acid, exercise caution; wear goggles and rubber gloves.) Rubber-base paint is truly waterproof and far more durable than latex, but it comes in flat and low-gloss finishes only and in a narrower range of colors, has a strong smell and is expensive. Because it is so tough, however, it is a good choice for basement floors. A coat normally dries in an hour. Rubber-base paints need special solvents; check the label carefully.

Any latex, oil or alkyd paint can be applied over a rubber-base paint, with one exception: a high-gloss oil paint will not adhere to this type of coating.

Cement Paint
RENEWS MASONRY SURFACES
APPLIED TO DAMP WALLS

This inexpensive coating gives a new surface to brick, stucco or concrete, adding a thin layer of cement to the old masonry. Some types also act as waterproofers —an advantage in basements. Two coats are necessary on new masonry.

The paint comes as a powder, which is a mixture of white Portland cement, pigment and, usually, a small amount of water repellent. This powder is mixed with water just before use and the paint is applied with a large brush. To help the cement set, the wall surface must be kept moist during the job and for at least 48 hours thereafter. Tools and spills must be rinsed off before the cement sets.

Cement paint forms a poor base for all other finishes.

Epoxy and Urethane Paints
VERY DURABLE
TRICKY TO USE

Plastic paints are exceptionally elastic and resistant to abrasion, grease, dirt and most chemicals. Although they are expensive, they may prove to be the best coatings for surfaces that are subject to chemical and physical stress—floors and steps as well as the walls and woodwork of kitchens and bathrooms.

In some respects the two types of paint differ. Urethanes can be used on bare wood or over latex, alkyd or oil paint. Epoxies produce a slick, impervious coating on nonporous surfaces such as ceramic or metal tile, glass, porcelain or fiberglass; they can also be used on concrete or wood floors, but they will not adhere to latex, alkyd or oil paint.

The most durable epoxies and urethanes are two-part paints, which must be mixed just before use because they dry and harden rapidly. Both types require special solvents, which are listed on the package labels, for cleanup.

Alkyd or oil paints can be used over an epoxy or urethane, but the surface must be roughened first by sanding.

Special Finishes

A number of unusual finishing paints are specifically designed to take care of special painting problems. They cost more and cover less than ordinary paints.

Multicolor Paint
DISGUISES FLAWED SURFACES
DISTINCTIVE AND DECORATIVE

These latex-base coatings contain two nonmixing pigments. Depending on the formulation, they produce a tonal variation or a flecked appearance that conceals uneven or slightly damaged surfaces. Multicolor paint can be used on any surface that takes latex paint. Choose a brand that can be brushed or rolled on and does not require spraying.

Any alkyd, latex or oil-base paint can be applied over a multicolor paint, but two coats may be needed to hide it.

Sand and Texture Paints
A COVER-UP FOR FLAWED SURFACES
ATTRACTIVELY ROUGH
DIFFICULT TO COVER

These paints dry to a rough rather than smooth surface that lends an unusual texture to walls and ceilings and also helps hide flaws. Sand paint is simply regular latex paint mixed with sand or a sandlike synthetic. It creates a fine-grained, glare-free texture that is attractive on ceilings but has a grittiness that limits its use to surfaces not likely to be touched.

Texture paint is an extra-dense flat latex or alkyd paint. To get an irregular, embossed texture, apply it to a small area at a time (page 39).

These paints can be applied to surfaces compatible with their latex or alkyd base. The latex type is often used on wallboard ceilings since it adheres without a primer and helps conceal seams.

Painting over sand or texture coatings presents special difficulties; their rough surfaces require as much as 25 per cent more regular paint than usual.

Dripless Paint
GOOD FOR CEILINGS
EXPENSIVE

This alkyd coating is prepared in a consistency so thick that it will not drip from a brush or a roller, making it useful for painting ceilings and high, hard-to-reach places. The thick paint will usually cover any surface in a single coat, but it is considerably more expensive than conventional alkyds and more of it is required to cover a given area.

Though this paint will not drip, it will spatter if it is carelessly applied; and its thickness makes it somewhat difficult to remove. Be sure to clean up tools and spills while they are still wet.

Fire-retardant Paint
A WORTHWHILE PROTECTION
AVAILABLE ONLY IN FLAT FINISH

This flat latex paint slows down the spread of fire inside a house by puffing up into a foamy insulating layer when exposed to high temperatures. The insulation helps to keep the paint film from flaring—as most paints will do—and also temporarily prevents flammable material underneath, such as wood studs and joists, from reaching the kindling point. Fire-retardant paint is particularly valuable in garages and basements.

Follow exactly the instructions supplied by the manufacturer, especially in controlling the thickness of the coating: if the coating layer is too thin, it will not provide adequate protection; if it is too thick, it may fall away in case of a fire. Some manufacturers suggest that their coatings not be washed because the puffing ingredients are water soluble; be sure to check the label.

Fire-retardant paints can be applied over any surface that is suitable for latex (and over bare wood, provided a perfectly smooth finish is not essential). Conventional paints should not be used over fire-retardant paint because they impair its effectiveness.

Transparent and Natural Wood Finishes

The clear finishes and natural colorings described below are generally used to protect or tone wood materials without hiding their desirable natural grain or texture, although they are occasionally applied over other surfaces as an extra coating. Except for bleach, all of these finishes should be applied with a brush.

Varnish
MOISTURE RESISTANT
TOUGHER THAN MOST PAINTS

Interior varnish is used chiefly to form a clear, tough finish for wood, especially floors and steps. Because it is exceptionally durable, it is also used on painted surfaces to protect the finish. For the correct way to apply varnish, see page 37. Most varnishes dry in a day, but are ready for a second coat in six to eight hours.

The basic types of varnish, in order of increasing durability, are: alkyd and phenolic, polyurethane, epoxy and moisture-cured urethane. The high-gloss versions are the most durable, but a medium-gloss varnish provides good protection. Scratches are hard to touch up, however, because new varnish forms a shiny patch on older varnish.

The alkyd and phenolic resin varnishes give a warm, glowing tone, but the others are much tougher; polyurethane varnishes are exceptionally resistant to alcohol and are useful for table and bar tops; epoxies can be applied to ceramic tile and other nonporous surfaces as well as raw or painted wood. Polyurethane and epoxy types come as ready-to-use liquids or in two materials, which must be mixed just before use. In each, the two-part mixture is more durable.

Moisture-cured urethane is the toughest of all interior varnishes. It can be used on ceramic tile as well as wood and other surfaces. It is expensive, however, and hardens best if temperature conditions fall within a restricted range.

Most paints do not adhere well to varnish, but oil or alkyd paints can be applied if the varnished surface is thoroughly roughened, first by washing with a strong detergent and then by sanding.

Shellac
INEXPENSIVE
FAST DRYING
EASILY DAMAGED BY WATER OR ALCOHOL

Shellac is an alcohol solution of a resin derived from the lac insect of the tropics. Either clear or reddish brown (called orange), it is an inexpensive, abrasion-resistant coating for bare, bleached or stained wood. It dries in two to three hours, depending on the weather, and it gives a mirror-smooth coating—brush marks disappear as the shellac dries. It is the traditional finish for wood floors.

These admirable qualities are balanced by disadvantages. Shellac cannot be used over other coatings because the alcohol in its base tends to dissolve the existing surface. Furthermore, it is easily damaged by water, which causes whitish spots to form, and by alcohol, which disintegrates the shellac.

Ready-mixed shellac, though convenient, soon loses its adhesiveness; check the date on the container to be sure it is not more than a month or two old. As an alternative, buy shellac in 4- or 5-pound "cuts" of natural shellac resin mixed together with 1 gallon of denatured alcohol. To thin this heavy material to a working consistency, add 1 gallon of alcohol to a 5-pound cut, or ¾ gallon to a 4-pound cut.

Stain
CHANGES WOOD TONE

Stain enhances the grain of wood by altering the color. Because it works by being absorbed into the wood pores, it must be applied to raw wood or to wood that previously has been treated only with sealer or bleach. After staining, the surface can be oiled, waxed or left bare, but generally it is coated with varnish in order to protect the wood and make it easier to clean.

Stains consist of varying amounts of pigment (the amount determines whether the final coat will be transparent or semiopaque) in oil, water or alcohol. Oil-base stains are most common. Stains with a water base penetrate more deeply than oil stains—an advantage if the surface is likely to be scratched—but the water raises the grain of the wood so that extra sanding is required. Alcohol stains dry faster than any other type—in 15 to 30 minutes—but fast drying can produce a streaky finish.

So-called double-duty stains, a combination of stain and varnish, change the color of the wood and simultaneously provide a protective coating. Use these mixtures with caution: they streak easily and are not as durable as ordinary stain covered with varnish.

Any paint can be used over a surface of oil-, alcohol- or water-base stain. If a wax has been used over the stain, remove this finish with a commercial wax remover or sand the surface down to the bare wood. If you are covering a double-duty stain, see "Varnish," above.

Bleach
LIGHTENS WOOD
REMOVES STAINS
CORROSIVE AND DANGEROUS

Raw wood that is too dark or discolored can be lightened with bleach. Bleach can also be used to correct a faulty staining job that has come out streaky or too dark. Caution: These chemicals are corrosive. Wear rubber gloves and protective clothing, protect eyes and wash away spatters immediately.

The most convenient bleach is simply undiluted liquid laundry bleach. Apply it to the wood with a rag or a stiff brush and scrub it in, then rinse it off thoroughly with warm water, sponging repeatedly to remove any trace of the bleach.

The bleaching and rinsing process raises the grain of the wood. After bleaching, let the wood dry, then sand it smooth and protect it with a coat of varnish.

Primers, Sealers and Fillers

A surface may be incompatible with the finishing coat of your choice. It may be so porous that the first coat will virtually disappear into it. Or it may be so uneven that no paint will give a smooth surface. The solution to these problems is to apply an inexpensive undercoat of one kind or another. Fillers will smooth a wood surface that is uneven and sealers close the pores of wood or masonry. Most common of all undercoatings are primers, which not only serve as the first layer on absorbent materials but also as a bridge between a finishing coat and an incompatible surface.

The primer for a flat finishing paint can be the paint itself, thinned with solvent (epoxies and urethanes are their own best primers). In most cases, however, using paint as its own primer is needlessly expensive. Ready-mixed primers are usually made with cheaper pigments and cost less than quality finishing paints. The ready mixes are thinner than finishing paints to promote quick drying, and they always have a flat finish to provide the rough surface, or "tooth," needed for good top coat adhesion.

Latex Primer
QUICK DRYING AND ODOR FREE
EASY TO CLEAN UP

This water-base primer is especially valuable in preparing plaster, concrete, gypsum wallboard or cinder block. Such masonry contains alkalis that destroy oil or alkyd finishing coats; the latex primer forms a barrier between the alkalis and the finish. In addition, this primer serves as a bridge between incompatible types of paint, since any paint will adhere to it and it will adhere to almost any surface —even to glossy oil paint if the surface is well sanded. Do not use it on raw wood, however: it will roughen the grain.

A latex primer has many of the advantages of latex paint: it is virtually odor free, it dries in two to four hours, and tools can be cleaned up simply with soap and water.

Alkyd Primer
BEST UNDERCOAT FOR WOOD
GOOD BASE FOR ALL PAINTS
NOT RECOMMENDED FOR WALLBOARD

An alkyd primer is the best undercoat for raw wood, because it does not raise the grain of the wood. Some primers of this type can be used on masonry. But it is not ideal as a first coat on gypsum wallboard because alkyd raises a slight nap on the wallboard's paper covering. Most finishing coats—including flat latex—adhere well to an alkyd base coat. Alkyd primers take overnight to dry; tools and spills can be cleaned with the odor-free solvents used for alkyd paints.

Metal Primer and Paint
PREVENTS PEELING AND RUST

In most homes, the metals commonly painted are steel and aluminum. Steel must be kept painted or it will rust away. Aluminum does not require painting, but it pits if it is left uncoated or exposed to weather. Either metal can be protected with a special primer plus a finishing coat or with a metal paint.

The best primer for steel is an alkyd or oil type containing zinc, which rust-proofs the metal. For aluminum, use a zinc-based oil or alkyd metal primer, or apply epoxy or urethane finishes directly to the bare metal as self-primers. Any compatible finish can then be applied over these primers. (When you apply a finish coat to a radiator, use flat instead of glossy paint, which blocks heat.)

Primer and top coat are combined in a single mixture in the so-called metal paints. These oil or alkyd paints come in high-gloss and semigloss versions and are available in a wide range of colors. They are applied by brush, and cleaned and thinned with the conventional solvents used for oil or alkyd coatings.

Copper, brass and bronze hardware are not normally painted; instead, the fixtures are usually lacquered at the factory to preserve their original appearance. If the coating wears away unevenly, clean the finish off completely with a lacquer remover. In the case of copper and brass, tarnish should be removed with fine steel wool and metal polish—or, for a mirror finish, metal polish alone—and a protective coating of polyurethane varnish or epoxy should be applied. Uncoated bronze develops an attractive patina that can be protected against abrasion with varnish; if bright bronze is desired, treat it like brass. To paint over these metals, use an alkyd metal primer containing zinc and any compatible finish paint.

All metal primers and paints must be applied to a surface that is absolutely free of dirt, grease and corrosion. Remove rust from steel with an abrasive such as fine steel wool and, if you are not using metal paint, be sure bare spots are touched up with metal primer. Clean off grease with paint thinner.

Sealers and Primer-Sealers
SEALS PORES OF WOOD AND MASONRY
PRESERVES NATURAL LOOK OF WOOD

These liquids, made of synthetic resins mixed with a high proportion of solvent, seal the pores of wood and masonry.

Transparent wood sealers sink into the pores, binding the fibers together and making them easier to sand. They protect wood against dirt and moisture but not abrasion. These sealers should not be confused with opaque primers or transparent shellacs and varnishes. They dry more rapidly than most primers, and unlike varnish or shellac, which leave a glossy sheen, they do not alter the appearance of the wood. Stain, oil, or alkyd paints or varnishes may be brushed directly over a clear wood sealer, since the wood, even though it is sealed, can absorb liquid.

So-called primer-sealers are opaque wood sealers (usually white) designed to solve a special problem: because they are resistant to wood resins, these sealers are brushed over wood knots to prevent the resin from seeping through a finishing coat. These sealers are often thinned with alcohol. Aluminum paint is also sometimes used as a stain sealer.

Clear masonry sealers—often tinted a translucent blue to make it easier to see the areas that have been coated—are used on concrete, cinder block or plaster to prevent chalking. Opaque masonry sealers are particularly effective at slowing water seepage through basement walls. All masonry sealers vary greatly in their composition; consult the label of the package for cleanup instructions and for compatible top coats if you intend to paint over them.

Wood Filler
SMOOTHS THE SURFACE
CAN BE MIXED WITH STAIN

Filling is an essential first step in attaining a really smooth finish on fine wood such as paneling. Though some painters skip this step when preparing paneling, a filler should always be used to smooth rough or damaged sections, and it will give good sections a satiny smoothness. Used alone, a filler preserves the natural look of the wood, but it can also be mixed with stain to fill and color wood in a single operation.

Filler, a combination of synthetic resins and a wood-toned pigment, comes in either paste or liquid form. The paste type is slightly thinned with turpentine (or with a special solvent recommended by the manufacturer) and the resulting thick liquid is brushed or troweled onto damaged surfaces or open-grain woods such as walnut, ash, oak or mahogany. Liquid filler, which is simply a prethinned paste, is generally applied to woods with a closer grain, such as maple or birch. Neither paste nor liquid filler protects wood; the filler should be supplemented by a coat of sealer and, in a surface subject to heavy use, a final coat of shellac, varnish or paint.

Tool Kit for Interior Painting

Like most jobs, painting requires both general-purpose tools and some that are more specialized. Have on hand a ruler, hammer, screwdriver, sanding block and clean rags. The more specific tools and materials shown here help you to do interior painting neatly, easily and efficiently.

☐ To protect furniture and floors from drips and spatters, use plastic or paper dropcloths. Lightweight plastic (½-mil to 2-mil gauge) will do for furniture; use a heavier gauge (up to 4 mils) for floors. Paper dropcloths are better than newspapers but not as good as plastic.

☐ For patching wallboard or plaster before painting, you will need both stiff- and flexible-blade putty knives, a 6-inch taping knife, a 10-inch smoothing knife and a roll of joint tape to close wallboard seams, and an ordinary beverage can opener to clean plaster cracks. Sandpaper smooths repairs, a sticky fabric called a tack cloth removes sanding and plaster dust, and a sponge cleans up dirt and washes down previously painted walls. For both painting and repairing you will need rubber gloves to protect your hands from solvents and caustic materials.

☐ Mixing paint calls for a medium-sized (one gallon) pail and either the mixing device that fits into an electric drill, or wooden mixing paddles.

☐ For the variety of painting situations you are likely to face, you need both rollers and several different brushes. Included here are a 3-inch flat brush with a beaver-tail handle for wide trim, flat areas, edges and corners; a chisel-edge brush; and angular and oval sash brushes for narrow trim and windows.

☐ Tools for rolling on paint include a roller tray, a grating for squeezing off excess paint, a roller cover, a 9-inch spring roller frame and an extension pole for ceilings and high areas.

☐ To protect nearby surfaces in precision painting, use masking tape, striping tape (used mostly for decorative work) and a triangular metal paint guard.

☐ Cleanup chores can be eased by a comb to clean and align brush bristles, a spinner to remove paint and solvent from rollers and brushes, and a window scraper to peel dried paint from glass.

SPONGE

TACK CLOTH

DROPCLOTHS

SANDPAPER

JOINT TAPE

CAN OPENER

PAINT GUARD

1¼" FLEXIBLE-BLADE PUTTY KNIFE

1½"-BLADE PUTTY KNIFE

6" TAPING KNIFE

10" SMOOTHING KNIFE

MASKING TAPE

STRIPING TAPE

3" FLAT
BRUSH

2" CHISEL-EDGE
BRUSH

ANGULAR SASH
BRUSH

OVAL SASH
BRUSH

ROLLER TRAY AND GRATING

ROLLER COVER

9" SPRING ROLLER FRAME AND HANDLE

BRUSH COMB

RUBBER GLOVES

WINDOW SCRAPER

PAIL

SPINNER

POWER MIXER

EXTENSION POLE

19

Before You Paint: Preparing Interior Surfaces

The success of any interior paint job depends largely upon the care with which the surfaces of walls and ceilings have been prepared before you apply the first strokes of a brush or a roller. Rendering these surfaces free of dirt, dust, grease or flaking paint, repairing cracks or holes, and sanding surfaces smooth are chores that must be done, and done correctly. If they are not, your new finish cannot form a strong, long-lasting bond with the surface. Fortunately for the home painter, the tools and materials for these critical jobs are few and inexpensive, and the skills are easy to acquire.

Before starting any preparatory work, make the surfaces accessible by clearing the room as much as possible. Move portable objects such as lamps, end tables and chairs out of the room, then cluster the bulky furniture and heavy rugs in the center and cover them with dropcloths (plastic dropcloths are best, but even old sheets will do). Take down drapes, curtains, blinds and pictures and remove the rods, nails and hooks that support them. Protect the floor or carpet by spreading newspapers along the baseboards and covering the papers and the rest of the floor area with more dropcloths.

Now inspect the surfaces thoroughly to determine the work you must do, and draw up a list of the equipment you will need. First of all, look for structural damage or defects that may call for professional repairs. Bulges, stains and areas of chalky powder, for example, indicate serious leakage within a plaster wall or ceiling; large holes in wallboard may require the replacement of pieces of board or entire panels. If the surfaces have been previously wallpapered or painted, try to ascertain if the material beneath the paint or paper is wallboard or plaster, and, on a painted surface, the type of finish that was used. Such information will determine certain specific preparation treatments, deglossing paint, for example, or removing powdery coatings such as whitewash (box, right) and will help you to select the proper undercoatings, primers and paints (chart, pages 8-9). Instructions for painting over wallpaper are on page 30, for painting interior brick on page 69, and for preparing garage and basement surfaces on page 64.

To complete your check list, go over the jobs that you must do. You may be lucky: if a surface is in good shape and the old paint is not loose or damaged, all that will be needed is a general cleaning (below). Far more often, however, surface preparation will include one or more of the following operations: stripping old wallpaper (pages 85-86); patching damaged plaster (pages 27-28); repairing punctures, concealing nails and taping joints in wallboard (pages 23-26); sealing wood knots (page 29); and scraping or stripping old paint (page 22).

Some paint scraping and patching will be necessary in almost all cases, and these chores present a few special problems. Choose your patching materials with care. Some brands contain asbestos, a potential cause of cancer and lung disease, and particles of asbestos are released when the dry forms of these patching materials are mixed with water or when the materials are sanded. It is not likely that their limited use for small home repairs is dangerous, but to be on the safe side ask for an asbestos-free spackling compound, wallboard joint cement or patching plaster.

Be equally careful in sanding patched or repaired areas—though here the caution is more a matter of procedures than of materials. Electric sanders or commercial hand sanders with fittings that grip the sandpaper firmly can be used, but all that is required for sanding small areas on interior surfaces is a homemade sanding block and a supply of medium- and fine-grit flint sandpaper or—slightly more expensive, but longer lasting—aluminum oxide paper. Work in a well-ventilated room, wear a respirator (page 55) if you are not absolutely sure that your patching materials are asbestos-free, and follow all sanding with a thorough dusting and vacuuming of the surface and surrounding area.

With all the equipment on your check list assembled, get to work. Surface preparation is a messy job, and cleansing agents, paint remover and sandpaper are either caustic or abrasive; therefore, wear old clothes, cover your head with a painter's hat or a scarf and protect your hands with gloves. Clean metal patching tools frequently so plaster or spackling compounds will not harden on them. Wipe them on newspapers, then wash with a wet cloth—do not rinse them off in a sink, because the compounds will clog the drains—and dry the tools thoroughly to prevent rusting.

The Importance of Cleaning

In every home, even the most immaculate, surfaces should be precleaned just before they are painted. Inevitably some dust or grease lodges on walls and ceilings—especially in bathrooms and kitchens—and on such dirt-catchers as baseboards, doors and door tops, and window trim. Every bit of dirt on any of these surfaces must be removed, for even fingerprints can prevent new paint from adhering firmly.

A good washing down with a heavy-duty household detergent will usually suffice for wall surfaces and for painted woodwork; a ceiling (which is less accessible) or an area of virgin wallboard (which would soak up water like a sponge) can simply be dusted or wiped with a mop. Any traces of water washes, such as calcimine or whitewash, should be scrubbed off with a stiff brush. An extra-strong solvent for dirt and grease is trisodium phosphate, or TSP, but because phosphates can pollute water supplies, TSP solvents are banned in many communities.

In addition to these general procedures, solve special problems as they arise. New paint will not adhere properly to glossy surfaces; dull such finishes by raising a nap—or "cutting a tooth," in painters' jargon—with sandpaper or a commercial deglosser. If floor wax has adhered to baseboards, take it off with wax remover. Remove rust (page 61) from radiators, pipes and heat ducts, and clean mildew from damp places (page 63). When stripping wallpaper, wash off remaining bits of paper, paste and sizing. Finally, always be sure that precleaned surfaces are completely dry before starting to paint.

Two Ways to Use Sandpaper

1 For a large, flat area. Make a sanding block from wood or corkboard. A block about 3 inches wide and 4 or 5 inches long will fit most hands comfortably. Cut a piece of sandpaper large enough to cover one surface of the block, with sufficient overlap so the paper can be wrapped completely around the block, as in the drawing at right. Wrap the paper with the grit side out.

SANDPAPER
SANDING BLOCK

2 Using the sanding block. Make sure that all loose paint is removed from the area to be sanded, and that any patching compounds are completely dry. Grasp the block firmly, holding the sandpaper snugly around it, and sand with a gentle, circular motion (*arrows*), ''feathering,'' or blending, the edges of old paint or patching materials into the surrounding surface. Tap the sandpaper frequently on a hard surface to remove accumulated residue, and replace the paper when it becomes clogged. In sanding previously painted surfaces, start with medium-grit sandpaper; for an extra-smooth finish, sand again with fine-grit paper wrapped around the block. When sanding virgin wood, use only fine-grit paper and do not use the circular motion; instead, work in straight strokes along the grain.

SANDING EDGE

3 For a hard-to-reach area. Angled or intricate places, such as corners, window trim or the indentations in moldings, are not easily accessible with a sanding block. To reach such spots, fold a 6-inch square of sandpaper into quarters to make a sharp sanding edge.

4 Using the sanding edge. Hold the folded sandpaper with the sharp main fold facing out, as in the drawing. Insert the fold into the area to be sanded—in this example, one of the wooden dividers in a window sash. Gently rub the paper over the surface, feathering the edges of old paint or patching material as you go. Refold the paper as necessary to make fresh edges.

Erasing Past Mistakes

A good paint job depends partly upon the care—or lack of it—exercised by previous painters. Careless painters leave heavy build-ups of old, brittle finishes, many layers of incompatible paints, and surfaces that are badly scarred—and these defects, in turn, create additional problems such as alligatoring, blistering and peeling (*pages 56-59*). These flaws must be corrected before you apply new paint, or the coating will not adhere and you will continue the cycle of failure.

To begin with, loose paint should be scraped off. If the process causes deep depressions in the scraped areas, the depressions must be filled in to level the surface (*top right*). More serious paint problems call for a different procedure: if the area of damaged paint is extensive or if many layers of paint must be removed, the old paint should be stripped off completely with a chemical paint remover (*bottom*).

Scraping Off Loose Paint

1 Removing the paint. For work on small areas, insert the edge of a 1¼-inch-wide, flexible or stiff-blade putty knife under the edges of loose paint (*drawing*) and, with a pushing motion, scrape off all the old finish that does not adhere firmly. For large areas, use a pull-type scraper (*page 54*) to save time. Be careful not to gouge the surface with either tool. (Caution: the pull-type scraper is comparatively difficult to control.) At the end of this phase, examine the surfaces to be repainted to be sure you have not overlooked any areas of loose paint.

PUTTY KNIFE

LOOSE PAINT

Stripping Off Old Paint

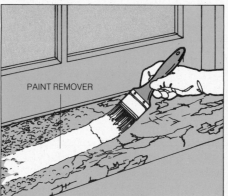

PAINT REMOVER

1 Applying paint remover. Use a water-washable, paste-type chemical paint remover for almost all surfaces. The exception to this rule is a surface covered with wood veneer, since a water wash may lift or buckle the veneer; use a benzine-based remover instead. All paint removers contain chemicals that are extremely caustic and can produce dangerous fumes; therefore, cover the surrounding area with a thick layer of newspaper, wear goggles, old clothes and rubber or plastic gloves, and be sure that the room is well ventilated.

Using a clean, inexpensive bristle paintbrush, spread a generous amount of remover on the area to be stripped (*drawing*). Work with short strokes, brushing in one direction. Do not cover an area more than 2 feet square at one time.

2 Filling in depressions. A minor scraping job may leave a slight, almost invisible depression between a scraped area and the edges of adhering old paint. In this case, feather (*page 21*) the edges of the old paint with sandpaper to blend them into the scraped surface. If the depression is deep enough to be noticeable, fill the low place with vinyl spackling compound or wallboard joint cement (*page 23*). Use a flexible-blade putty knife to apply the filler to a small depression; use a wide-blade wallboard taping knife (*page 10*) for extensive filling (*drawing*). When the filler has dried, sand it even with the surface. Spot-prime (*pages 8-9*) all scraped or filled areas before repainting.

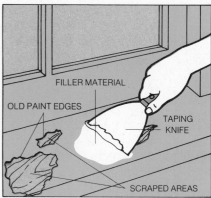

FILLER MATERIAL

OLD PAINT EDGES

TAPING KNIFE

SCRAPED AREAS

OLD PAINT

2 Removing the paint. When the paint begins to blister and wrinkle, peel it off with a taping knife (*drawing*) or a stiff-blade putty knife. As you remove the paint, clean the knife frequently by wiping it on sheets of newspaper. Then apply the remover to the next area. If one application is not sufficient, brush on as many coats as necessary, but always peel off the loosened paint between each coat of remover. When all paint is off, follow the instructions on the paint-remover label to clean the bare surface, using a wash of water or benzine as the label directs. Wait for the surface to dry, then smooth it lightly with fine-grit sandpaper.

Making Repairs in Wallboard

The material most often used today for constructing, or making major repairs in, walls and ceilings is gypsum wallboard, also called plasterboard or dry wall. Wallboard is made in standard 4-by-8-foot panels, consisting of a core of calcined gypsum (a form of plaster) sandwiched between layers of strong paper. Usually, a panel is fastened to wall studs or ceiling joists with special ridged nails. The slightly indented joints between the panels are concealed by a perforated paper tape overlaid with a patching and filling compound called joint cement.

There are good reasons for the widespread use of wallboard. It is cheaper than plaster, can be put up faster and is less likely to develop cracks or holes. Moreover, a homeowner can, with little experience, install or repair it himself. But wallboard has its disadvantages, too. It is easily punctured, and because of expansion and contraction as weather conditions change or a house settles, the taped joints between the panels my open up and the nails holding the board in place may pull, or pop, away from the surface. Instructions for solving these problems begin at right and continue to page 26.

The preparation of wallboard, like that of plaster, is relatively simple, and the same rules apply: the board must be smooth, clean and dry. However, if you intend to paint brand-new wallboard, it must be sealer-primed with latex-base paint (page 14), since solvent-thinned primers will raise the nap of the paper covering. (Oil paint may be spread on top of latex.) Spot-prime all patched areas on previously painted wallboard with a thinned version of the finish coat.

The equipment for working on wallboard consists of a taping knife, which resembles a putty knife but has a broader blade; an ordinary hammer, which has a slightly rounded face; a roll of perforated wallboard joint tape; and a can of premixed joint cement.

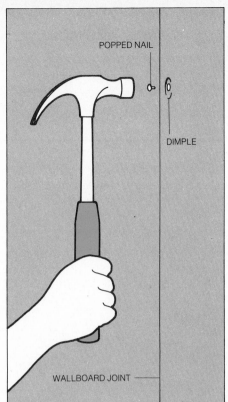

2 Patching the dimples. Apply a thin, smooth layer of joint cement over the dimpled nail with a taping knife (drawing). Let the cement dry (its color will change from dark to light beige). Add a second layer of joint cement slightly larger than the first. Be sure there are no rough spots, especially at the edges.

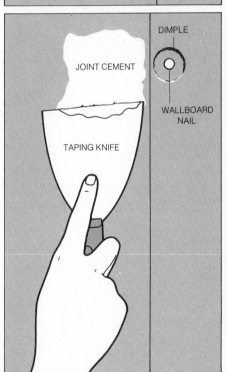

Reseating Popped Nails

1 Securing and dimpling the nail. Popped nails may occur at any point where a panel is attached to a wall stud or a ceiling joist, and the nailhead may be covered or partly covered by tape and joint cement. The remedy is the same in all cases. Hold the hammer squarely over the nail (drawing) and strike the head firmly to drive it flush with the surface. Then tap the nail gently to embed it a fraction of an inch below the surface, so that the rounded face of the hammer creates a small depression, or dimple, in the surrounding wallboard without breaking the surface. (A driven and dimpled nail is shown to the right of the joint in the drawing.) If the nail still pops slightly, countersink it with a nail set (page 30) and insert a new nail 2 inches directly above or below. Dimple the new nail as you did the old one before going on to Step 2.

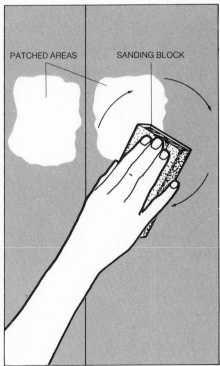

3 Leveling the surface. When the patched areas are completely dry, smooth them with fine-grit sandpaper. Sand gently, with a circular motion. If you are working on new wallboard, be careful not to raise the nap of the paper covering. Feather the edges of the patches (page 21), and complete the job by dusting the patched areas.

Taping Wallboard Joints

1 Filling the joints. The procedures on this page apply both to sealing new wallboard joints and to repairing damaged ones. One extra step is necessary on an old joint: remove loose or damaged tape and crumbled joint cement from the area you plan to reseal. Starting at the end of a new joint or the edge of the damaged area on an old one, spread a ⅛-inch-thick layer of wallboard joint cement directly over the joint with a 6-inch-wide taping knife. (If the blade of the knife is too wide to be inserted into the can, spoon some cement onto the lid of the can or any clean, shallow container.) Press the knife firmly against the wallboard to force the cement into the joint. Throughout this procedure, when applying the cement, use long, smooth strokes.

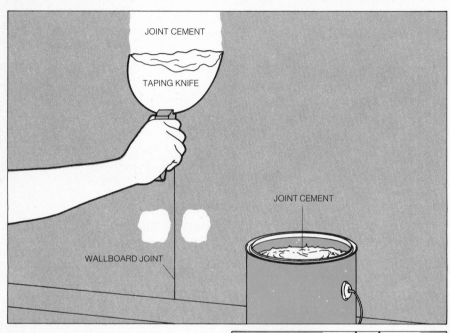

JOINT CEMENT

TAPING KNIFE

JOINT CEMENT

WALLBOARD JOINT

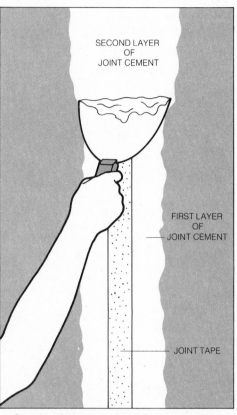

SECOND LAYER
OF
JOINT CEMENT

FIRST LAYER
OF
JOINT CEMENT

JOINT TAPE

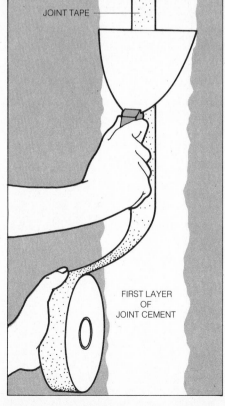

JOINT TAPE

FIRST LAYER
OF
JOINT CEMENT

2 Applying the tape. Hold a roll of perforated joint tape in one hand and a taping knife in the other. Center the tape over the joint and, with the knife at a 45° angle to the wallboard, draw the knife blade over the tape to embed the tape into the cement. If the tape wrinkles or veers away from the joint, lift it up carefully and recenter it.
When repairing a short section of an old joint, slightly overlap the ends of the undamaged tape with the new tape, then tear the new tape from the roll. If you are taping the full length of a joint between wallboard panels, apply about 2 feet of tape at a time (do not break or tear the tape), until you have covered the entire joint.

3 Covering the tape. Apply a thin, smooth layer of joint cement over the newly affixed joint tape. Use enough cement to extend this second layer an inch or so beyond the edges of the first layer of cement *(drawing)*. At the end of this step, check to be sure that the tape is completely covered by the second layer of cement, that this second layer is as smooth as you can make it, and that all excess cement is evened out, especially at the edges of the layer. Then let all the cement dry completely. Unless the weather is humid, the cement should dry in about 24 hours.

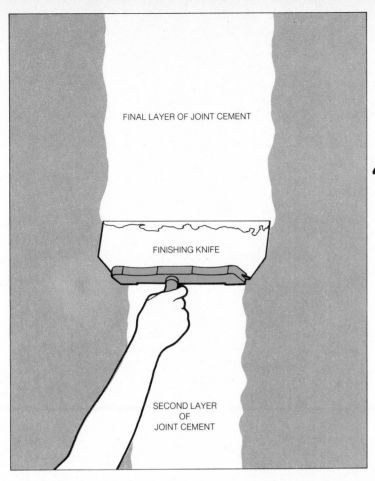

FINAL LAYER OF JOINT CEMENT

FINISHING KNIFE

SECOND LAYER
OF
JOINT CEMENT

4 **Applying the final coat.** After the first application of cement and tape has dried hard, smooth on a very thin finish coat of joint cement in a layer about 10 to 12 inches wide. (To make it easier to apply this wide layer, you may decide to purchase the 10-inch-wide finishing knife shown in the drawing, but the 6-inch-wide taping knife used in Steps 1 through 3 will also do the job.) Remove all excess cement at the sides of the finish coat, so that the cement tapers off gradually onto the wallboard. Once again, let the cement dry, then sand the cemented area with fine-grit sandpaper wrapped around a sanding block, feathering the edges *(page 21)*. If you are working on new wallboard, be especially careful not to sand the surface next to the joint cement or you may damage the wallboard's paper covering.

Filling Holes

1 **Small and large jobs.** A tiny wallboard hole can be filled with ready-mixed vinyl spackling compound and sanded smooth. A larger hole, up to 1 inch wide, should first be stuffed with a wad of newspaper, cover the paper with patching plaster and let the plaster set. Add a layer of spackling compound or wallboard joint cement; when dry, sand the surface smooth. The procedure on this page is designed for still larger holes, from 1 inch to about 6 inches wide. (A hole that is bigger than 6 inches should not be repaired with plaster; instead, use a piece of new wallboard.) First, remove the loose or torn wallboard around the opening. Cut a piece of wire screen that is slightly larger than the hole, thread a length of string through the screen and set the screen inside. Moisten the inside edges of the hole with water and apply patching plaster to the moist edges with a putty knife; make sure that plenty of plaster projects inside, behind the wallboard.

Now curl the screen's edges and fit it through the hole *(drawing)*. Insert the screen all the way into the hole. Pulling the ends of the string gently, draw the screen flat against the inside of the hole and embed it in the fresh plaster.

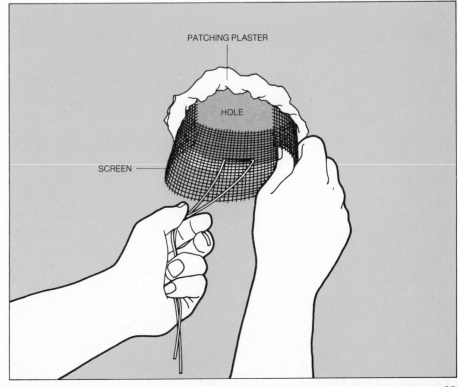

PATCHING PLASTER

HOLE

SCREEN

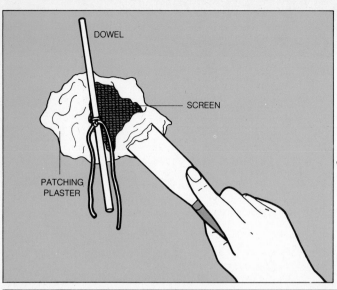

DOWEL

SCREEN

PATCHING
PLASTER

2 **Initial filling.** Secure the screen to the back of the hole by placing a dowel or a similar piece of wood across the opening and tying the ends of the string firmly around it (*drawing*). Fill the hole with plaster to a level almost—but not quite —flush with the wallboard surface. Cover all portions of the screen around the dowel, then turn the dowel slightly to increase tension on the screen. Let the plaster set for about a half hour.

3 **Removing the dowel.** When you are sure that the patching plaster has set, remove the dowel by cutting the string as close to the plaster as possible (*drawing, below*). A spot of bare screen will be exposed where the dowel was tied; wet the dried plaster around the spot with water and fill the spot with fresh plaster until the screen is completely hidden. Now cover the entire patch with a second layer of plaster to bring it flush with the wallboard surface. Allow this plaster to set.

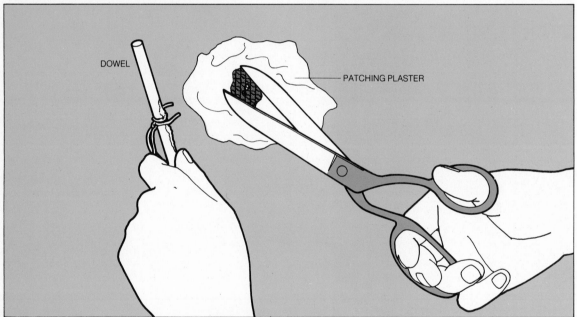

DOWEL

PATCHING PLASTER

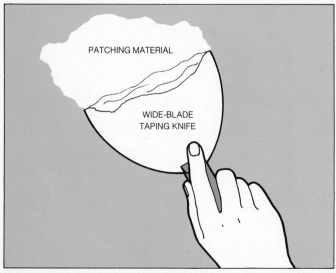

PATCHING MATERIAL

WIDE-BLADE
TAPING KNIFE

4 **Final sealing.** When the plaster has set, cover the patched hole with wallboard joint cement or ready-mixed vinyl spackling compound (both are easier to sand than patching plaster), using a wide-blade taping knife. Extend the layer of patching material slightly beyond the edges of the patch, so that it covers a little of the surrounding wallboard (*drawing*). Spread the material evenly and smoothly with slow, steady sweeps of the knife, and remove any excess. Let the patching material dry for about 24 hours. Finally, sand the patch with fine-grit sandpaper wrapped around a sanding block (*page 21*).

Patching the Faults in Plaster

If you live in a home built before World War II, walls and ceilings are likely to be plaster, applied in two or more layers over a lath backing of wood, metal or gypsum. Plaster is as easily prepared for painting as wallboard, since small cracks, holes and irregularities are simple to fix; major repairs to large areas, however, require considerable skill, and in some cases, the services of a professional.

Do not be timid in attacking the problem. Cracks and holes need some enlargement for a neat repair. And the best approach to a large and unsightly bulge is to take a hammer and knock out the humped plaster, then treat the hole you have made as you would any other hole. A shallow depression is built up with several thin layers of vinyl spackling compound or wallboard joint cement. When the spackling compound or cement is dry, sand it smooth, blending its edges into the surrounding plaster until the area that was damaged is flush with the surface of the wall.

If the old plaster around a repaired spot was deliberately stippled or left rough, use a stiff brush, sponge or comb to duplicate the texture on the patching material while it is still damp. To match a sandy texture, fill the hole almost to the top with plaster, apply a latex primer to the patch, then cover it with a layer of sand paint *(page 39)*.

Repairing a Hole

1 Preparation. With a putty knife, chip any loose or crumbling plaster from the edges of the hole until only solid plaster remains. (Caution: If you find seriously damaged lath underneath, the lath must be repaired before replastering; repair generally calls for the skills of a professional.)

Repairing a Crack

1 Cleaning. With the tip of a beverage can opener, scrape away crumbling or loose plaster along the edges of the crack. The drawing shows a hairline crack being widened a fraction of an inch to make a larger surface for patching material to adhere to. A wider crack would require undercutting as described in Step 2 on page 28. Lengthen any crack slightly by removing a bit of the firm plaster at each end. This helps the patching material grip the sound surface, and keeps the crack from extending farther in the future. Vacuum the cleaned crack or, with your eyes shut, blow out the plaster dust.

2 Sealing. Using a clean paintbrush, wet the inside of the crack and a little of the surrounding area with clear water. With a flexible-blade putty knife, spread wallboard joint cement or vinyl spackling compound along the entire length of the crack in a long, smooth ribbon, pressing the material in firmly. Be sure that the patch overlaps some of the solid plaster surfaces along the edges and at both ends of the crack. Let the patching material dry for a day or so; if it shrinks add another layer. When the material is completely dry, smooth it with fine-grit sandpaper, wrapped around a sanding block.

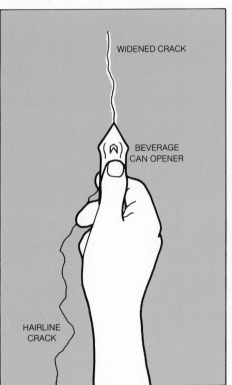

WIDENED CRACK

BEVERAGE CAN OPENER

HAIRLINE CRACK

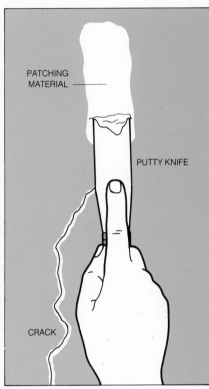

PATCHING MATERIAL

PUTTY KNIFE

CRACK

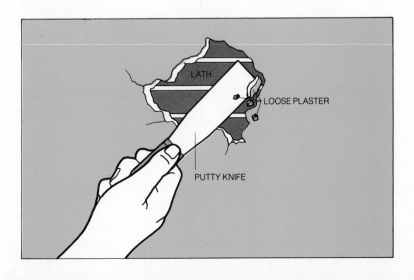

LATH

LOOSE PLASTER

PUTTY KNIFE

2 Undercutting. All holes in plaster (and all cracks wider than ⅛ inch or so) must be undercut, a procedure in which some of the old—but intact —plaster is removed along the inner side of the hole (or crack) so that the patching material that is used as a filler will bond securely to the solid plaster around the opening. To undercut, use the tip of a beverage can opener and scrape away a bit of the plaster under the rim of the hole. Then bevel the scraped area to make a V-shaped hollow under the surface. Vacuum or blow out the plaster dust from the undercut area.

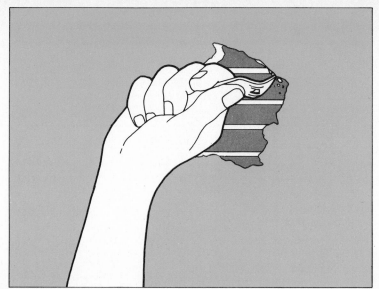

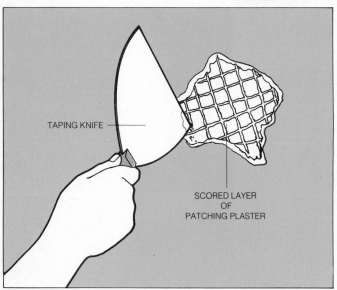

TAPING KNIFE

SCORED LAYER
OF
PATCHING PLASTER

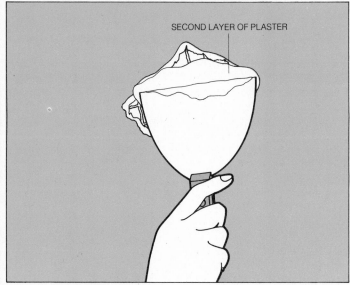

SECOND LAYER OF PLASTER

3 Applying the first layer. Mix enough patching plaster to fill the hole almost completely. Moisten the back and edges of the hole with a sponge. Beginning at the undercut surfaces at the edges of the hole, apply the patching plaster with a taping knife. Continue to fill the hole until the patching plaster is about ¼ inch below the surface of the undamaged plaster around the hole. While the patching plaster is still wet, score its surface with the tip of the taping knife (*drawing, above*). This scored surface will provide a firm grip for a second layer of patching plaster. Let the first layer set for about a half hour.

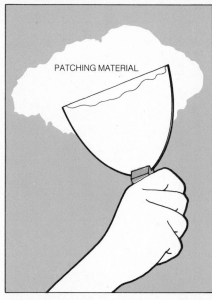

PATCHING MATERIAL

4 Applying the second layer. Mix a fresh batch of patching plaster. Dampen the scored layer of patching plaster and 2 or 3 inches of the undamaged surface around the hole. Using a taping knife, preferably wider than the hole, fill the hole with plaster to the level of the undamaged area, spreading the plaster onto the surrounding surface for an inch or so. Smooth this layer by drawing the knife blade evenly over the patched area. Let the plaster set.

5 Completing the patch. Cover the filled hole with a smooth layer of wallboard joint cement or vinyl spackling compound, using a taping knife (*drawing, left*). Continue spreading the cement or spackling to an inch or so beyond the edges of the patching plaster. Let the patched area dry for several days. When completely dry it will feel hard and will have lost the clammy feel of wet plaster. Sand the dry area smooth with a sanding block and feather the edges of the compound (*page 21*) into the surrounding surface.

Correcting Wood Problems

Almost every room will have some wood surfaces—window trim, built-ins, doors, moldings—that you may want to paint along with the walls and ceilings. Generally, you will be working on a previously finished surface, and if you are lucky the only preparations needed will be a thorough cleaning with detergent and remover to take off grease, dirt and wax, and possibly deglossing a previous high-gloss paint *(page 20)*.

Frequently, though, you will need to make some repairs, such as countersinking nails or closing joints *(page 30)* and sealing knots *(right)*. On moldings and other areas that receive little or no abrasion, fill depressions or holes with vinyl spackling compound if you are going to apply paint; if you are planning to stain or varnish the surface, use water putty mixed with a water-soluble color that matches the wood. On doors and other areas that are often touched or handled, use plastic wood filler, which is tougher than spackling compounds. Sand down old paint drips and defects such as cigarette burns. Scrape off all loose paint and level any deep depressions with spackling compound or wood filler. If the damage is extensive, strip the paint down to the bare wood *(page 22)* and then sand it thoroughly.

Bare wood, whether or not it had once been painted, must be sealed so that paint will form a film upon the surface. Use the appropriate primer or, if the wood is porous, coarse-grained or deeply gouged, a paste wood filler.

On both painted and bare wood, follow repair work with a careful, thorough sanding. Always use fine-grit paper and, on bare wood, sand with the grain. Dust a surface immediately after sanding it, then just before painting, dust it again. To pick up the finest residue, use a tack cloth. They can be purchased but are easy to make for yourself. Slightly dampen a clean cotton cloth with water, then apply an ounce or two of turpentine and the same amount of varnish. Work the fluids into the cloth as you apply them, wringing the cloth out as necessary, until they are evenly distributed and the cloth is yellowish and barely damp.

Loose or Oozing Knots

Sealing and sanding. If wood knots are oozing resin—which will leave a sticky lump under any finish—scrape off hardened resin with a sharp knife *(drawing, above)*, then clean the area with turpentine or other paint solvent. Seal the knot with thinned shellac *(above, right)*; when dry, sand lightly. If the knot is loose, remove it with long-nose pliers. Fill the hole with plastic wood filler; sand, then apply shellac, sanding again when dry. If the knot cannot be removed and it is flush with the surface, seal it with unthinned shellac. Sand lightly when dry. If the knot protrudes, build up the surrounding area with plastic wood filler; sand and seal as described above.

Popped Nails and Open Joints

1 Countersinking a nail. Use a nail to set to countersink a finishing nail that has worked so loose that its head has popped away from the wood surface. Place the nail set over the nailhead, with the shaft perpendicular to the surface *(drawing)*. Strike the set sharply with a hammer to embed the head about ⅛ inch below the surface.

2 Spackling a nail or joint. With a flexible-blade putty knife, fill the slight depressions over countersunk nails with vinyl spackling compound, water putty or plastic wood filler, depending on the surface you are working on *(page 29)*. Also, check all wood joints, especially around window- and doorframes. If shrinkage or warping has caused a joint to open slightly, fill with the proper patching compound *(drawing)*, roughly shaping it to match the molding contours if the crack is wide. Let the compound dry, then check it for shrinkage and add more if needed. Sand the dried patches with fine-grit paper to smooth them and complete shaping contours.

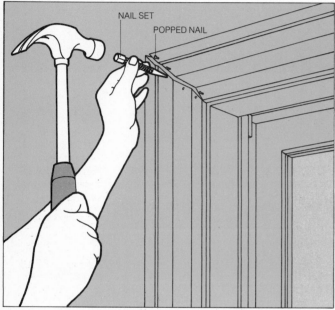

NAIL SET
POPPED NAIL

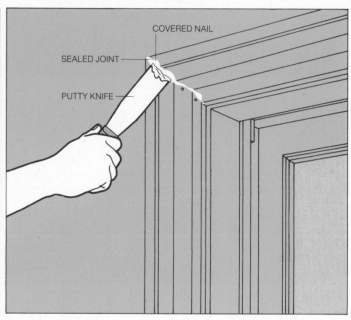

COVERED NAIL
SEALED JOINT
PUTTY KNIFE

Painting Wallpapered Surfaces

The problem of painting over wallpaper calls for special caution and a healthy skepticism: it is not always possible to paint over wallpaper. A vinyl- or plastic-coated paper, for instance, simply will not hold paint. The design of a textured paper will show through the paint. If you paint over several layers of any wallpaper, the weight of the layers plus the weight of the paint may cause both paint and paper to fall off the wall. Paint can also soften the adhesive holding a paper to the wall.

Yet in spite of the arguments against painting upon wallpaper, you may want to do just that. If you have wallboard underneath your wallpaper and if you suspect that the wallboard has not been primed or sized, you really have little choice: wet-stripping the paper may se-

riously damage the paper covering on the wallboard. In other situations, you may be unwilling to tackle the messy and time-consuming job of stripping most types of wallpaper.

If, for whatever reason, you do decide to paint a wallpapered surface, observe these three basic principles: the paper must adhere firmly to the wall, it must be clean and grease-free, and any imperfections in it must be repaired. Instructions for cleaning wallpaper are given on page 121. For specific repairs, see pages 118-121 for regluing loose paper, patching holes and fixing blisters. For wall preparation and stripping techniques, see pages 84-87.

To patch areas of torn or missing wallpaper, first glue down any loose paper. Then cover the area with two thin lay-

ers of a vinyl spackling compound, applied with a wide-blade taping knife —extending the compound slightly beyond the edge of the damaged area. When the compound is dry, sand the patch so that it is flush with the surrounding wallpaper, working gently to avoid raising the nap of the paper.

Check for bruises that may indicate there is damage to the wall itself. To repair such damage, follow the directions on pages 23-26 for wallboard and on pages 27-28 for plaster surfaces.

Finally, test the paper for color stability. Brush a little of the paint you plan to use on an unobtrusive spot, then wait a few days to see if the dyes of the paper bleed through the paint. If there is discoloration, seal the wallpaper surface with shellac before you paint.

A Room Wrapped Up and Ready for Painting

The room below indicates the range of repairs and preparation that may be required before painting begins. Most of the repairs, such as patching cracks and holes or sealing wood joints *(pages 20-30)*, will be necessary only from time to time. Any properly prepared room, however, should bear some resemblance to this mosaic of swatches and patches.

A lot of the precautions you took before making repairs (such as covering the furniture with dropcloths) will serve equally well as protection against the inevitable splattering of paint. Minor paint splashes on hardware or glass are not serious; if you catch them before the paint dries they are easily removed with water or chemical solvent and a clean rag. If, however, you are a perfectionist—or you want to save time when cleaning up—a few simple, last-minute tasks that will result in a neater job are suggested:

☐ OUTLETS AND SWITCHES. Unscrew the fuses or turn off the circuit breaker for the room. Remove the switch and receptacle plates, then group them together *(lower left);* paint the plates when you paint the walls. Sand off any chipped paint around the openings. Turn the electricity back on for illumination if necessary, but paint carefully around the openings and keep children and pets away.

☐ LIGHTING FIXTURES. Loosen the attaching screws of the mounting plates of the ceiling fixtures *(top center)* or the wall sconces *(right)* so that the plates stand away from the surface a bit. In painting, use a brush to cut in carefully around the rims of the mounting plates. Protect the fixtures by covering them with plastic bags or sheets of plastic fastened with masking tape, and do not turn on these lights while the plastic is in place.

☐ STATIONARY APPLIANCES. Use newspaper or plastic secured with masking tape to cover air conditioners and radiators *(below windows)* or thermostats *(beside light switch).*

☐ HARDWARE. Uninterrupted surfaces are always easier to paint, so some painters remove as much hardware as possible —unless, of course, the objects themselves are to be painted. You may wish to take off items such as doorknobs, the plates behind them and cabinet handles. Masking tape will protect parts not easily removed, such as door hinges, locks and striker plates. Window-sash locks can either be removed or masked.

☐ WINDOW GLASS. Many painters use the beading technique *(page 37)* on window sashes and dividers, but you may wish to protect the panes with masking tape, leaving a $1/16$-inch gap between the tape and the wood or metal window parts.

Final preparations. After repairs are completed, you may find that the area to be painted looks worse than before, but the new paint will rapidly cover all of the patched surfaces. Before starting to paint, you may wish to attend to some of the protective measures suggested above.

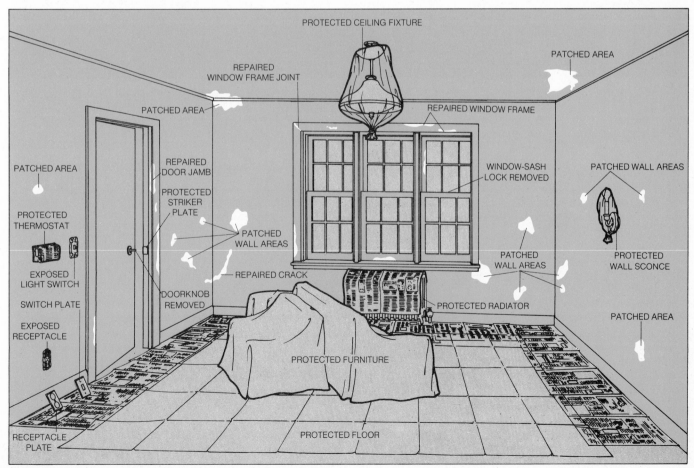

PROTECTED CEILING FIXTURE

PATCHED AREA

REPAIRED WINDOW FRAME JOINT

REPAIRED WINDOW FRAME

PATCHED AREA

PATCHED AREA

REPAIRED DOOR JAMB

WINDOW-SASH LOCK REMOVED

PATCHED WALL AREAS

PROTECTED STRIKER PLATE

PROTECTED THERMOSTAT

PATCHED WALL AREAS

PROTECTED WALL SCONCE

EXPOSED LIGHT SWITCH

REPAIRED CRACK

PATCHED WALL AREAS

SWITCH PLATE

DOORKNOB REMOVED

PROTECTED RADIATOR

PATCHED AREA

EXPOSED RECEPTACLE

PROTECTED FURNITURE

RECEPTACLE PLATE

PROTECTED FLOOR

Fine Points of Applying Paint

The basic rule for easy, efficient interior painting is simple: Use a roller whenever and wherever you can. In recent years even professional painters have been abandoning their cherished brushes for ceiling and wall work, and with good reason. A roller covers these areas more than twice as fast as a paintbrush and requires less skill and effort. Guidelines for picking a good roller and for matching a roller to a specific surface appear on the opposite page.

A roller alone, however, will probably not suffice for the whole job. Most interior painting calls for a combination of roller and brush; a single brush, as a matter of fact, may not be enough for the most efficient work. You need a brush for surfaces that a roller is not designed to cover—a delicate, ridged molding, for example, or the narrow divider between windowpanes. You also need a brush —not necessarily the same brush—to use in corners that a roller cannot reach. And you may turn to a brush to paint certain flat areas, such as the wall above a built-in cupboard, where working with a roller is awkward.

Choose a brush of the right size and shape for the kind of work you are doing. Use as wide a brush as possible, to make the painting go faster, but not wider than the surface you are covering. A 1- or 1½-inch trim brush is good for window dividers, a 2- or 2½-inch sash brush for baseboards and window frames and sills. For large, flat areas use a 3-inch or, at most, a 4-inch brush. (Professional painters regularly use 4-inch or even 5-inch brushes, but it takes long practice and a powerful wrist and forearm to handle them with ease.)

Choose a brush shape that is tailored to the job, using the pictures on page 19 as a guide. The familiar flat brush with squared-off ends is a general-purpose brush; for precise edges and lines, pick a flat trim brush with a beveled, chisel-shaped working end. An angular sash brush, especially designed for certain hard-to-reach surfaces, cannot normally be used on flat surfaces but is ideal for the insides of window- and doorframes or the louvers of a shutter. Round or oval brushes have the largest paint-carrying capacity and splay out when applied to a surface; they work best on thin, curved surfaces, such as pipes.

Finally, match your painting tools to the type of paint you are using. Latex paint, which is likely to be used for at least part of every job, calls for a brush or roller with synthetic bristles or nap. Natural bristles and fibers absorb water from latex paint and loose their resiliency. For oil or alkyd paints, which give a smooth gloss to trim, professionals have long preferred a finely tapered hog-bristle brush. However, a good synthetic-bristle brush will also do a fine job and can also double as a cutting-in brush if you are using latex on the rest of the room.

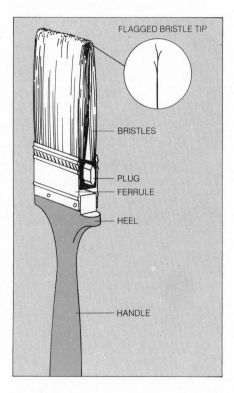

Designed for flow. This cutaway shows the desirable elements to be found in a typical flat brush. The bristles, whether natural or synthetic, are "flagged"—that is, split or frayed—at the working end to provide greater area for holding paint. At the other end, the bristles are embedded in hard plastic. One or more "plugs," or spacers, made of metal, wood or hard rubber separate the bristles where they are embedded (you can see a plug by separating the bristles with your hand). The bristles along the sides of a plug "toe in" and meet at the tip in a firm, trim edge from which paint flows evenly. A metal band called a ferrule holds the bristle base to the heel of the handle.

FLAGGED BRISTLE TIP

BRISTLES

PLUG

FERRULE

HEEL

HANDLE

What Makes a Good Brush Good?

When you are shopping for a paintbrush, carefully check the points that are listed below. These guidelines apply to both synthetic and natural-bristle brushes of any size and shape, and can help you to make a knowledgeable on-the-spot appraisal of quality.

☐ Grip the handle of the brush as you would for painting *(page 36)*. The shape and the weight should feel comfortable in your grasp. The metal ferrule should be attached solidly to the handle, preferably with nails. If the handle is made of wood, it should have a glossy or rub-berized coating, which resists moisture and is easy to keep clean.

☐ Press the bristles against the palm of your hand. They should not separate into clumps but should fan out slightly in an even spread. When you lift the brush away from your hand, the bristles should readily spring back to their original position.

☐ Examine the bristles with care. They should be smooth and straight and the tips should be flagged, as shown in the drawing above. If you are comparing brushes that are the same width, select the one with the longest, thickest bristles; it will hold the most paint.

☐ Part the bristles and examine the way they are set into the base. The plug or plugs should be no more than half the thickness of the setting.

☐ Slap the brush against the palm of your hand to shake out any loose bristles—any brand-new brush may have a few. Then tug on the bristles once or twice. No additional bristles should come out. If any do, be wary; badly anchored bristles will seriously hinder the efficiency of the brush.

Picking the right roller. Both the cover and the frame of the roller below have features worth looking for when you choose a roller. The cover wraps in a spiral around the central core (if it is not made this way, ridges will appear in the painted surface). The core itself is plastic; plastic-coated cardboard is almost as good, though less durable. The frame has a spring cage that holds the core firmly in place (cheaper models, with frames that do not support the middle of the cover, may quit working effectively long before a job is done). Nylon bearings at the end caps of the frame help the cover turn smoothly. The handle is contoured for a comfortable grip, and the end of the handle is threaded to accept an extension pole.

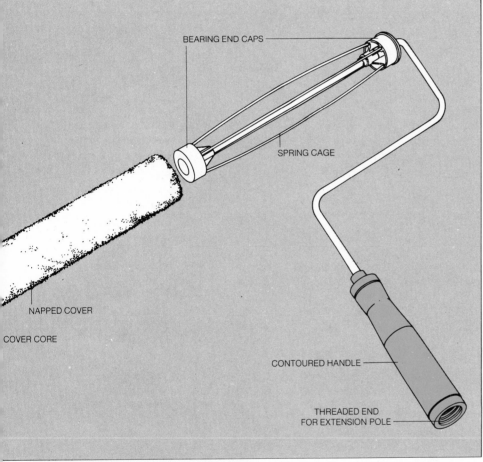

BEARING END CAPS

SPRING CAGE

NAPPED COVER

COVER CORE

CONTOURED HANDLE

THREADED END
FOR EXTENSION POLE

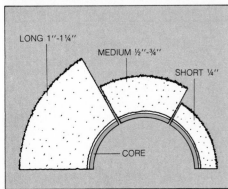

LONG 1″-1¼″

MEDIUM ½″-¾″

SHORT ¼″

CORE

Fitting a nap to a paint and a surface. Roller covers are sold in short, medium and long nap lengths. A short nap, generally about ¼ inch deep, does not hold as much paint as the others but is the best kind to use with glossy paint, since it leaves a thin, very smooth coating. The all-purpose medium nap, about ½ to ¾ inch deep, holds any type of paint well and produces a soft-looking, stippled effect. The deep pile of a long nap—about 1 to 1¼ inches—works a heavy load of paint into the irregularities of a textured, damaged or extremely porous surface, and can be used to create a deeply stippled effect on any surface.

Protecting Yourself —and Your Pets

Remember that when you paint you are using strong chemical mixtures, and must take proper precautions.

☐ Water-thinned paints, such as latex, are the safest, but like all coatings they contain poisonous ingredients. Keep them out of the reach of children.

☐ Use special care in handling paints based on mineral spirit (oil and alkyd types); these paints are highly flammable and their fumes are toxic. Do not be misled by the fact that you may not smell any fumes; the new "odorless" types are just as flammable and poisonous as the ones you can smell. Do not use mineral-thinned paints in a poorly ventilated room, and do not drink alcoholic beverages when you paint with them; alcohol can so increase your body's susceptibility to some fumes that the inhalation of even a small amount may be fatal. Never rest a can of paint on a kitchen range; as an additional precaution, check the manufacturer's label to see whether a paint or thinner is so flammable that the pilot light of a gas range should be extinguished.

☐ When painting a ceiling or getting at a high spot on a wall, do not handle the roller or brush so that you risk getting paint in your eyes.

☐ Do not leave any coating on your skin longer than you must; wash up carefully every time you quit.

☐ The label on a paint can always lists specific antidotes. Keep the label on hand in the event that you need to call a physician.

☐ All too frequently, curiosity-prone pets find ways of getting into your painting area—and into your paint. The results may seem comical, but paint on an animal's skin and fur can do serious harm unless you remove it before the animal starts licking it off. Wash off latex paint with plain water. To remove oil or alkyd paints, soak a cloth with mineral oil or cooking oil and use it to slide the paint off the fur or skin. Never use turpentine or any other powerful paint solvent: it will burn the animal's skin and will be doubly dangerous if it is licked off.

Mixing and Straining

Most of a mixing job is generally done for you by the paint dealer, who will give paint a vigorous shake by machine when you buy it. Then if you use it within a day or so, all you have to do is give it a few turns with a mixing paddle.

If the paint you bring home has not been machine-agitated, however, you are likely to find a thin, colorless fluid on the surface and a thick layer of pigment at the bottom of the can. To restore such paint to its proper consistency turn it upside down, tightly sealed, and let it sit that way a few hours or, better still, overnight. Before you remove the lid, shake the can vigorously. Then open the can and follow the steps shown at right.

Plan to use a second container for the actual painting, especially if the original can is gallon-sized. Use a little paint at a time from this auxiliary pail, and keep the big can closed, so that the paint inside is less likely to dry out, get dirty or spill.

Manual mixing. Pour about one third of the thin paint at the top of the can into a second container. Stir the remaining paint to a uniform consistency, using a wooden paddle. Do not use a metal spoon or piece of wire; the inside of a paint can has a rust-preventing coating that might be damaged by metal scraping against it. Gradually add small amounts of the thin paint that was poured into the container back to the can, stirring as you add each portion (*drawing*), until all of the original contents of the can have been returned to it. Pour the mixed paint from the can to the container and back again several times for a final, thorough blending.

Power mixing. A variable-speed electric drill with a two-blade mixing attachment like the one below stirs up a badly settled can of paint quickly. Submerge the mixer in the full can of paint until both blades are under the surface. Since power mixers are usually made of metal, which can scar the coating of a paint can, do not operate your mixer with the shaft near the sides or bottom of the can. With the drill off, lower the mixer until it touches bottom, then raise it to a position in which a couple of inches of paint-covered shaft show above the surface of the paint, and turn on the drill to a low speed. To avoid splatters, turn off the drill before withdrawing the mixer.

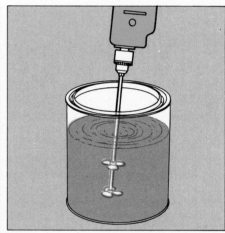

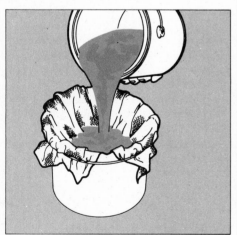

Removing paint skin. If a can of oil-base paint has been opened and then resealed carelessly a thick skin of hardened paint may form on the surface. Do not plunge a paddle or mixer into the skin; this tough layer never dissolves, and attempts to mix it with the rest of the paint will leave stray bits that show up on a newly painted surface. To remedy this problem, gently separate the skin from the side of the can with a paddle. Drape cheesecloth over a separate container and tie the cloth to the rim with string (*drawing*). Pour all of the paint through this filter and then discard the cheesecloth and paint debris. Mix the remaining paint as described above; it is not affected by the loss of the material in the skin.

Mixing in color. Creating a special color for more than a gallon of paint is beyond the skills of most amateurs; you will find it almost impossible to match batches that are mixed separately. Rely instead on the wide variety of premixed colors, or ask your paint dealer to mix as much as you need in the shade you want. If you want to experiment with color-mixing, however, to create a new shade or match an old one, use the concentrated tint called universal colorant, which comes in many colors and works with all types of paint.

Do not mix the colorant directly into the full can of paint, for the smallest error can ruin a whole batch of paint. Instead, pour a small amount of

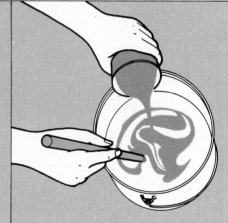

paint into a clear plastic or glass cup. Using the guidelines on the colorant label to estimate the correct proportions, add the tint to the sample of paint in the cup and stir (*above*). The clear cup allows you to see whether any of the unblended color adheres to the sides.

When the color in the cup is thoroughly mixed, begin adding the tinted portion back to the original paint a little at a time, stirring slowly by hand until you have reached the exact shade you want. If you are adding color to sand paint, allow the paint to stand for about half an hour after you have added the color so that the colorant will be absorbed evenly by the particles.

Avoiding Lumps and Drips

Once the paint has been mixed and you are underway, time-consuming interruptions should be kept to a minimum. The best intentions and the steadiest hand cannot ensure against the drip that sticks to the newspapers on the floor, and that then sticks to the furniture or to your shoe. Stray bristles, dust and other debris find their way into your paint bucket and eventually onto what you hoped would be an unblemished surface. Correcting these little annoyances can take up more time than applying the paint. The following suggestions can help keep these distractions to a minimum, making the job neater and quicker and the results more satisfactory.

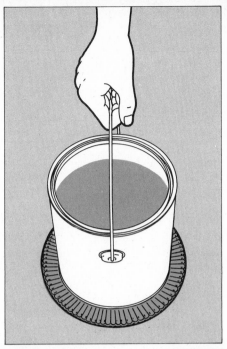

Drip-proofing the can. To cut down on paint splashes on your floor, make a drip guard for your paint can from a plastic-coated paper plate; attach it to the bottom of the can with masking tape, doubled over so it is sticky on both sides. The paper plate catches all of the drips from the edge of the can, and when you move the container the drip guard travels right along.

Keeping the paint clean. Stray bristles, hardened pieces of paint and bits of dirt that inevitably get into your paint can mar the work and are nearly impossible to fish out. Solve the problem another way. Before you begin to paint, cut several pieces of screen wire to the size of your paint-pail opening. Then, when something falls into the paint, drop a screen onto the surface. It will sink, taking debris to the bottom and trapping it there.

Preventing an overflow. The U-shaped rim of a paint can often becomes an overflowing reservoir of paint. To avoid drips from gallon cans, hammer a small nail several times through the bottom of the rim, making holes around the circumference. Paint that is caught in the rim will then drain back into the can, which can still be sealed for storage because the lid covers the holes.

Thick latex paints may clog the holes quickly, so keep a nail handy to open them up again. This draining technique cannot be used with cans smaller than a gallon because nailing holes through the narrow rim of a small paint can may skew it so badly the can cannot be resealed.

The Basics of Brushwork

The first step in brushwork starts before a drop of paint is deposited on a surface. To begin with, you must hold the brush correctly; your work will be neater and less tiring. A sash-and-trim brush like the one pictured at right is generally used for beading, cutting-in and a variety of jobs on flat surfaces such as doors. Its long, thin "pencil" handle is most effectively grasped with the fingers, much as you would hold a pencil or a fork. This grip provides the greatest control for careful work. A long-handled brush will enable you to adjust your grip for reaching into close areas, and to switch easily from one hand to the other.

Wider and heavier brushes for larger wall areas, like the one below, usually have stout handles, a type called "beaver tail." This handle provides balance for the heavier bristle bunch but is too thick to be gripped comfortably with the fingers, pencil-style. A beaver-tail handle is best held firmly with the whole hand, as you would hold a tennis racket. With all flat brushes, whatever their handle style, you may want to switch for a change of pace to the grip used for beading *(opposite, bottom),* with your thumb on one side of the ferrule and your other fingers on the other.

Loading the brush. Dip bristles into the paint one third to one half of the way up from the tip. Then tap the ferrule of the brush gently against the rim of the pail to remove excess paint. Do not wipe the brush across the pail rim because that removes too much paint. And do not overload the brush by dipping it in too far. The excess will drip off or run down into the heel and over the handle; if the paint collects and dries inside the ferrule, it will ruin the brush.

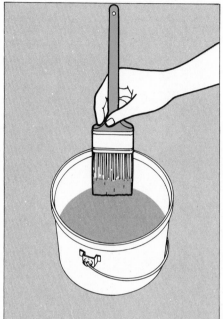

A fine, feathered brushstroke. If you are using the appropriate brush with the right paint, you need apply very little pressure as you paint. Each brushstroke should be about double the length of the bristles of your brush. The stroke begins with the flat side of the brush angled low to the surface (1). As you move the brush, the angle will increase gradually (2). Wherever possible, end each stroke in the wet paint of a previously painted section, drawing the brush up and off the surface with a slight twist (3); the brush should leave a thin, feathered edge of paint that will merge into a smooth layer of new paint.

Most initial brushstrokes are upstrokes, like the one shown below. Follow it with a downstroke over the same area or, if a single stroke covers the area satisfactorily, over the area at the immediate right or left. Continue brushing until you have covered a small section of the surface.

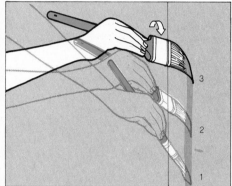

PAINT SHIELD

Painting in sections. When you paint an area considerably wider than your brush, such as the space above a built-in cabinet or below a window, work in rectangular sections. The size of a section depends largely on the setting speed of your paint and the capacity of your brush. With fast-setting paints, cover small sections, each about two brush widths across and two bristle lengths long; experiment with somewhat larger sections when you are working with medium- or slow-setting paint. Start a new section about two brush lengths below a completed one, and work toward and into the area of wet paint *(drawing).* Work vertically whenever possible; up-and-down strokes are the least tiring.

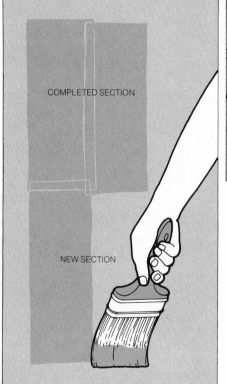

COMPLETED SECTION

NEW SECTION

Guarding as you go. A triangular metal or plastic paint shield, available for a few cents from paint dealers, is used by many painters to protect surfaces adjoining the area being painted. It works best on trim such as baseboards, where there is a fine crack separating the two areas. The guard can then be forced into the crack so that no paint gets on the edge of the shield, where it might cause smears. Hold the shield with one hand over the surface to be protected, push its edge into place and paint with the other hand. Wipe the shield clean frequently, or it will make more smears than it prevents; and do not use an improvised cardboard shield, which will soon become soggy and shapeless.

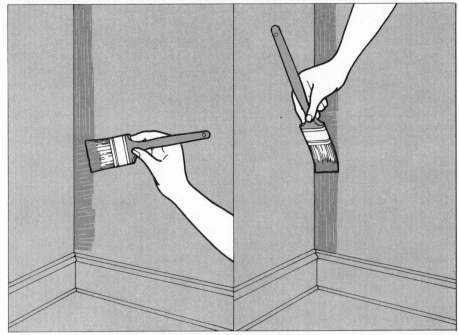

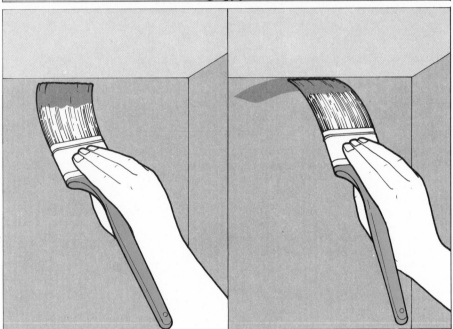

Cutting in. Even when you paint a room with a roller, you must first use a brush to cut in—that is, to paint a strip about 2 inches wide in corners between two surfaces of matching paints and colors. (Do not use the technique described here when you are painting ceiling and walls in different colors, or woodwork and walls in different colors or paints; instead, use the more precise beading technique shown below.) To cut in, take four or five overlapping brushstrokes perpendicular to the edge of the wall (*far left*) or ceiling, then smooth this strip with one long stroke that ends in an area of wet paint (*left*). Leave a 1/16-inch space when you begin the perpendicular strokes near the baseboard, then smooth the paint all the way down when you begin your long stroke.

Beading. You can achieve a steady, straight edge where two colors meet, or paint the narrow dividers between windowpanes without the bother of masking tape, once you master a brush technique called beading. Use a trim brush with a firm chiseled bristle edge (*page 19*). Grasp the brush on the heel with your thumb on one side and all four fingers on the other. Press the brush flat against the surface, forcing a thin line of paint—the bead—to float along the bristle tips (*far left*). Then, in one smooth, steady motion, draw this paint bead along a line about 1/16 inch from the edge of the surface you are painting (*left*). The wet paint will spread out sufficiently in all directions—including the vertical one—so that it draws even to the line itself.

Varnish: A Clear Exception

The rules for applying varnish and other clear, fast-setting coatings are quite different from those for ordinary painting. Some manufacturers provide special instructions on can labels, but most clear coatings are applied by the following method:

Load the brush up more than you do with regular paint, dipping the bristles into the varnish for about half their length. With each brushload make one long, smooth stroke rather than several short, overlapping ones. (Repeated brushing creates bubbles on the surface that cannot be eliminated.) Instead of painting from a dry to a wet area, start each new stroke at the end of the previous stroke. Most jobs require at least three coats of varnish, with a light sanding between coats.

The Basics of Rollerwork

Rollers need no special preparation unless you are using glossy paint and a new, fluffy short-nap roller. In that case, prime the roller by sloshing it in soapy water to remove loose strands of material. Rinse thoroughly and make sure the nap is completely dry before you begin.

A roller pan can be used just as it comes, but you will find it easier to saturate the roller evenly if you insert a specially made wire-mesh grating, such as the one in the drawing at right, over the sloped side of the pan. Cleanup is simplified if you line the pan before each use with heavy-duty aluminum foil.

For most rooms, a 4-foot extension handle is all you will need to reach high places. Before you buy any extension, however, see if the threaded end of your push broom, mop or wax-applicator handle will fit into the roller handle.

Loading the roller. Crimp a sheet of aluminum foil securely around the rim of the pan. Fill the well of the pan half full and dip the roller in. It will be a little less than half submerged. Lift the roller and roll it down the sloped grating—but not back into the paint. Roll on the grating two or three times. Dip the roller into the paint once more and roll it on the grating until the cover has been saturated evenly. Do not overload the roller or it will drip and slide, producing an uneven coat.

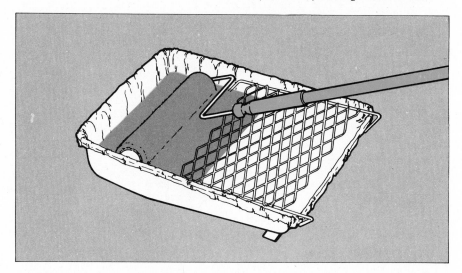

Starting with a Zigzag

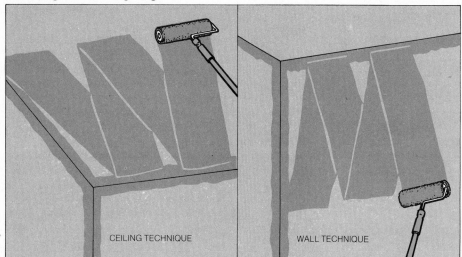

CEILING TECHNIQUE

WALL TECHNIQUE

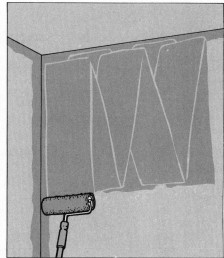

1 Patterns for ceilings and walls. To paint a ceiling, begin about 3 feet from the corner and roll toward the corner—the first stroke with a newly loaded roller should always be away from you. Then continue, without lifting the roller from the surface, to make a "W" pattern about 3 feet square, as in the drawing above.

To paint a wall, push the roller upward on the first stroke—away from you—and then complete an "M" pattern (center drawing). These initial strokes spread the heaviest part of the paint load evenly over the section you will now fill in (right) without removing the roller from the surface.

2 Filling in. After completing an "M" or a "W," begin filling in a 3-foot square by crisscrossing strokes of the roller without lifting it from the surface. Each stroke should be about 18 to 24 inches long. Use even pressure to avoid bubbles and blotches, and stop when the entire section is evenly covered with paint. There is no need to finish up with uniform strokes all going in one direction. Move along to the next section, load the roller again and repeat the sequence by making an initial pattern and then filling in.

Creating a Texture Effect

Texture paint has the consistency of wet plaster and can be fashioned to produce a rough, rustic surface or more formal patterns. A similar product, called sand paint, is mixed with coarse granules that give it a gritty appearance. Both paints are usually used to cover walls and ceilings that have small cracks, bumps or poorly concealed wallboard joints.

Preparation of the old surface is still important, however. Peeling paint must be scraped off but you need not be so meticulous about smoothing over patches because the paint texture will obscure many of the irregularities.

Plain texture paint should be put on with a trowel, a wide brush or a wide sponge-rubber applicator like the one used here. Sand paint can be applied with a long-napped roller or a wide, stiff synthetic-bristle brush.

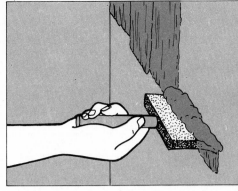

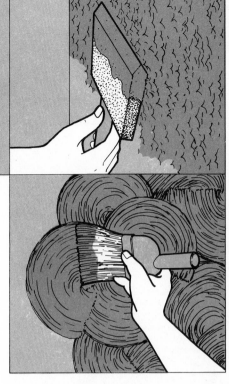

Stippling and swirling. To apply texture paint, smear it onto the surface as evenly as possible until you have covered a 3-by-3-foot section with about 1/16 inch of paint. Work your texture pattern on that area before covering another section. The sponge-rubber applicator shown here doubles as a texturing tool. When you pat the flat side of the tool over the surface, tiny peaks rise up that give a deeply stippled effect (*above, right*). An ordinary sponge or a piece of crumpled wax paper produces a similar effect. For more formal patterns, draw a plastic whisk broom lightly over the wet paint in straight or wavy lines or, as in the drawing at right, in a series of overlapping arcs.

Taking a Break

When you suspend a painting project for more than a day you need the kind of major cleanup described on pages 44-45. When you break for a shorter time—a few minutes to overnight—take the following simple precautions.

☐ If you are certain to resume painting within 15 minutes or so, leave your brush on a support—never standing on its bristles in a can. The support at right is coathanger wire run through two holes in the top edge of a pail.

☐ For a longer break, wrap wet brushes or rollers in plastic wrap or aluminum foil (*right, below*). Do not bind the bristles or nap too tightly. Set brushes on their sides or hang them by the handles.

☐ If you have paint left in your roller tray or in an open pail, cover it tightly with plastic or, better still, pour the contents back into the original can and reseal by hammering the lid down.

☐ For an overnight break there is no need to clean the rim of a resealed can before you tap the lid in place. But to avoid splatters, toss a cloth over the lid before you tap.

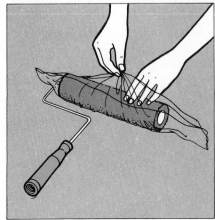

The Sequence for Painting the Parts of a Room

For the beginner, interior painting can be a botched affair of smeared paint and drips on newly finished surfaces. But it need not be. To avoid such problems, professionals have worked out a systematic approach.

Paint a room from top to bottom: the ceiling first, then walls, then windows, doors and other woodwork, and, finally, the baseboards. First "cut in" 2-inch-wide strips with a brush around the edges of the ceiling, using the technique described on page 37. Then switch to a roller with a 4- or 5-foot extension pole and, starting at a corner *(drawing, below)*, paint a section about 3 feet square. Continue to cover the ceiling, working across its shortest dimension in 3-foot-square sections, covering each section with one dip of the roller. With this technique you can do the job faster and more easily from the floor than if you use the brush. Also, by overlapping each newly painted area with one that is still wet, you will avoid the lap marks made when the wet paint is laid over dry.

If the room is very small or the ceiling surface is heavily textured, you may decide to paint all of the ceiling with a brush. Paint small sections with each dip of the brush—the size of each section will depend on the size of the brush *(page 36)*—and continue across the room section by section. Once you have begun to paint the ceiling, either by brush or by roller, work steadily across the short dimension as shown.

Walls are painted in much the same way. Starting at the ceiling, cut in with a brush. Use the brush also to cut in wall-to-wall corners and the edges of windows, doors, baseboards and cabinets. Then paint the walls in a way comfortable for you. Many people prefer to paint in vertical portions from top to bottom. However, if you are using a roller on an extension pole, you may find it easier to work horizontally across the wall in 3-foot-square sections; then remove the extension from the roller and continue painting across the room. This sequence saves the bother of removing and replacing the extension pole as you paint each strip down the wall. Paint each wall without stopping, then pause for a careful look at your work. While the paint is still wet, cover missed spots with a thin layer of paint.

Painting double-hung windows in the sequence shown opposite will solve the tricky problem of moving the sashes to paint surfaces that are obstructed by the lower sash. Paint the horizontal parts of the frame with back-and-forth strokes of the brush and the vertical parts with up-and-down strokes.

To minimize drips on the glass panes, hold a metal or plastic splash guard over the pane about ⅛ inch away from the wood. Do not, however, rely on this shield for a straight edge; instead, use the beading technique shown on page 37, and apply the paint 1/16 inch onto the glass to make an airtight seal. To clean any paint smudges or drips, use the scraper technique described on page 45.

Painting doors, cabinets and drawers is a relatively routine chore, although doors present a few special problems. There is one conventional rule: the latch edge and the hinge edge should be painted the same color as the room into which the edge faces when the door is open. Remember, too, that when you paint a brand-new door—one that has never been painted before—you should take it off the hinges to get at the bottom edge; otherwise moisture may be absorbed through the unsealed edge to cause warping. Remove the lower hinge first; otherwise the door may fall off the upper hinge and its full weight may ruin the bottom hinge. Tap the pin gently from below, using a punch and a hammer if necessary. When the pin has lifted a half inch or so, grip it just below the head with pliers and tap the pliers until the pin has been extracted.

Ceilings and Walls

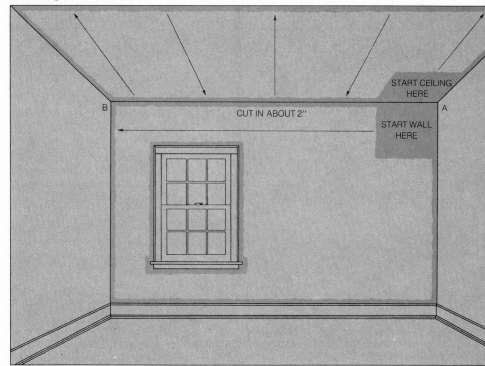

CUT IN ABOUT 2"

START CEILING HERE

START WALL HERE

B

A

A basic pattern. Face the long dimension of a room, as in the diagram above, and start the ceiling at corner A or B. The arrows trace the paths to follow if you start at A; reverse their directions if you start at B. Shaded areas indicate where you must use a brush to cut in paint. When you reach a door or window, cut in the entire frame at once, rather than segment by segment.

Double-hung Windows

1 **Starting on the sashes.** Raise the inside sash and lower the outside sash until their relative positions are almost completely reversed, as shown. To avoid getting in your own way, paint the inside sash in this order: inner strips (horizontals and then verticals), outer strips (horizontals and then verticals). Do not paint the top edge of the inside sash; you will use that surface to move the sash for the next step. On the outside sash, paint the same parts in the same order as far as they are exposed—but do not paint the bottom edge. Paint this edge when you paint the house's exterior.

2 **Completing the sashes.** Pushing against their bottom and top edges, move the outside sash up and the inside sash down to about 1 inch of their closed positions. In the same order as in Step 1, paint the surfaces of the outside sash that were obstructed; also paint the top edge of the inside sash. Now paint the wood framing of the window in this order: top horizontal, the two side verticals, then the sill. Wait until all of the paint is thoroughly dry before painting the wooden parts of the jamb *(Step 3)*; in the meantime, if there is another window in the room, work on it.

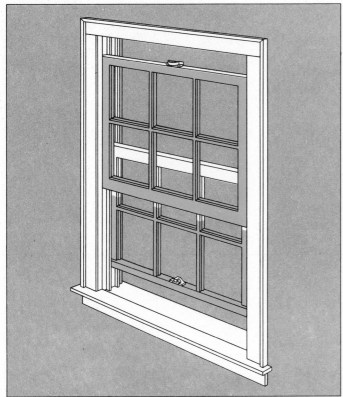

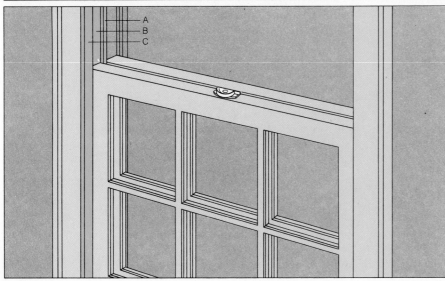

3 **Finishing with the jambs.** When the newly painted parts of the window are dry to the touch, move both sashes up and down a few times to make sure they do not stick. Then, push both sashes down as far as they will go to expose the upper jambs *(left)*. Metal parts are never painted. Paint the wooden parts of the upper jambs in the order shown by the letters A through C. Use a light touch to prevent paint from flowing down into the grooves of the lower jamb. Let the paint dry thoroughly, then raise both sashes as high as they will go and paint the lower halves of parts A through C. Again, wait for the paint to dry before lubricating the channels with paraffin or silicone spray to ease opening and closing.

Casement Windows

Choosing a primer and paint. Casement windows may be made of aluminum, steel or wood. An aluminum window need not be painted at all, but to protect the metal against dirt and pitting, some owners coat it with a metal primer or a transparent polyurethane varnish. A steel casement should be coated with both a metal primer and paint, or with a paint especially suitable to metal, such as an epoxy or polyurethane paint. A wood window should be treated like any other interior woodwork. Before painting a wood casement, open the window. Working from inside outward and always doing horizontals first and then verticals, paint the parts in this order: inside strips, outside strips, hinge edge, frame and sill. Leave the window open until all the paint dries.

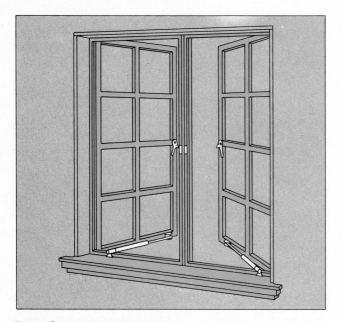

Doorframe and Jamb

Opening in or opening out. Paint the top of the doorframe, then the two sides. Next, paint the part of the jamb between the frame and the doorstop. If the door opens into the room you are painting (*drawing, left*) paint only the side of the doorstop that directly faces you (*blue*). If the door opens into the next room, paint both the side of the doorstop that directly faces you and the side that is adjacent to it (*right, green*).

Hinged Doors

Starting at the top. When repainting a door surface as part of a room renovation, open it wide to reach all of the parts to be covered. Always work from top to bottom. If the door is paneled, paint the panels first, the horizontal sections next, and finally the vertical sections. If the door opens into the room you are painting, use the same color on the latch edge that you have used for the rest of the door. If it opens into the next room, do not paint the hinged edge; it should be the same color as the other room. If the hinges have never been painted, it is preferable to leave them that way; to protect paint from spattering on the metal, cover the hinges with masking tape. The top and bottom edges of a door need be painted only once in its lifetime, to seal the wood.

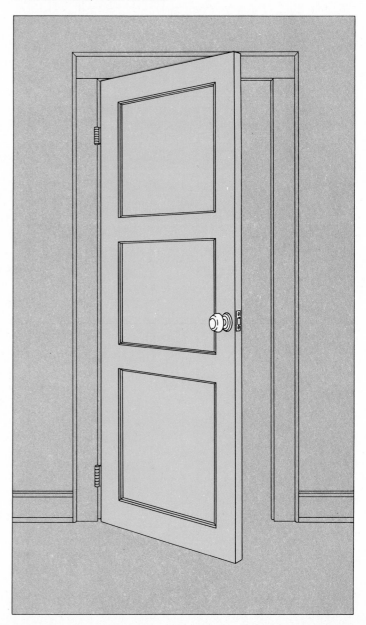

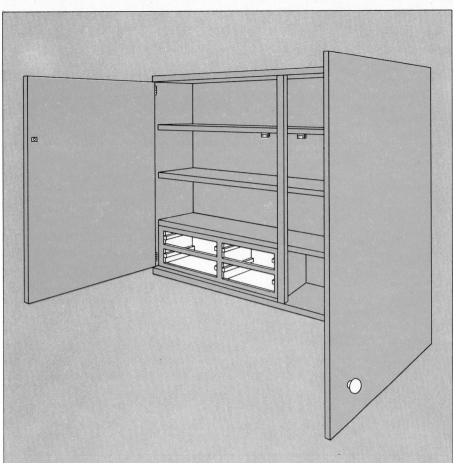

Cabinets and Drawers

Starting on the cabinet. Remove all drawers entirely before you begin to work; they will be painted later. Paint the cabinet (*drawing, left*) working your way systematically from inside to outside. Paint the walls first, then the shelves, then the door. When painting the shelves do bottoms first, then tops and edges. The outside surfaces are painted from top to bottom.

Drawers (*below*) need only their fronts painted. Do not paint the bottoms or exterior sides—paint there would prevent smooth sliding. For the same reason, do not paint the cabinet interior into which the drawers fit. If you wish to paint the insides of drawers for cleanliness or appearance, paint the sides first, then the bottom.

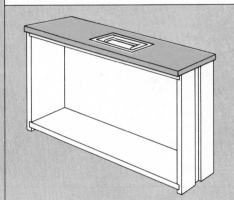

Sequences for Louvers

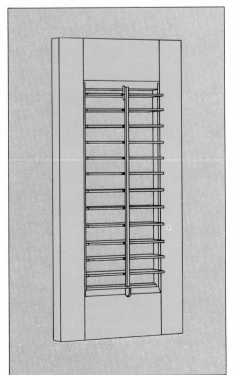

Solving the slat problem. The narrow slats of a louvered shutter or door are difficult to paint and call for special techniques. Use a ½-inch brush and a slow-drying oil or alkyd paint, so that you have time to brush in and smooth drips on these slats. To avoid paint build-up at the corners of a slat, start painting at one end of the slat, flowing the paint onto the wood in a long, smooth stroke. Start the next stroke at the opposite end of the same slat and flow the paint toward the wet area.

To paint an adjustable louver, open the louver wide and set the slats to a horizontal position. Cover as much of the slats as you can reach from the side of the louver opposite the adjusting rod, painting the slats first, then the frame.

Turning to the side of the louver with the adjusting rod (*drawing*), paint the inner edge of the rod, then wedge a small stick (a matchstick will do) through one of its staples to keep the rod clear of the slats. Finish painting the slats, one by one, smoothing out all paint drips as you go. Next, paint the outer edges of the frame, then the other parts of the frame. Complete the job by painting the rest of the adjusting rod. The slats of a stationary louver are set in a fixed, slanted position; therefore you will have to work the brush into the crevices between slats, then smooth out the paint with horizontal strokes. Follow the same sequence as for an adjustable louver, starting at the back so that you can catch and smooth out paint drips from the front.

Completing the Job: Cleanup and Storage

The correct cleanup for a paint job begins very early—in fact, before the first can of paint is opened. When you move furniture out of the way and cover floors with newspapers and dropcloths, you are spared the job of removing paint smears and spatters later. With these preliminary preparations done, the cleanup afterward is limited to removing paint from your tools and putting them away, storing leftover materials safely, and restoring order to the room.

Always clean paint from containers and applicators before the paint has a chance to dry. Begin by pouring unused paint from buckets and trays back into the original cans. Then wipe as much paint from the containers as possible with dry paper towels. Squeeze excess paint from brushes and rollers by drawing them across sheets of newspaper.

The procedure for removing the rest of the paint from your tools is relatively simple for water-thinned paints, somewhat more complex for solvent-thinned ones. If you have been painting with water-thinned latex products, simply rinse most of the paint with running water, then wash away the last traces with dishwashing detergent. A paintbrush comb like the one shown at right helps dislodge paint from the part of a brush near the ferrule. Use paper towels to dry buckets and trays; the inexpensive centrifugal device shown on the opposite page dries brushes and rollers much faster and more thoroughly than paper towels.

If you have been using a solvent-thinned paint, clean trays and buckets by wiping them with paper towels dampened with such solvents as turpentine, benzine or mineral spirits; the manufacturer's label will recommend a specific solvent for the paint you have used. Brushes and rollers must be agitated in a container of solvent to remove paint residue. Coffee tins make good containers for cleaning brushes; tennis-ball cans or loaf pans work well for rollers (if you have trouble finding an appropriate container for a roller, clean it in its own tray). Pour enough solvent to cover a roller completely or to reach the ferrule of a brush, then twist and pump the brush or roller to help dissolve paint lodged deep in the bristles or nap. Use a paintbrush

comb at this stage to clear paint from the area near the ferrule.

Replace the solvent as soon as it becomes saturated; use two or three changes of solvent, if necessary, until the brush or roller scarcely tints the liquid. Remember that solvents are flammable and that their fumes are toxic. Do not smoke while using them, do not use them near an open flame and be sure that ventilation is adequate to disperse the fumes.

Blot up the excess solvent from your equipment with paper towels or by spinning the tools briefly, wash everything in warm, soapy water to remove the last traces of solvent and paint, then dry all containers and tools thoroughly. A brush should, if possible, be hung by a hole in the handle for this drying stage; a roller should be set on end.

After the final wash and dry, buckets and trays are stacked in a closet or under a workbench. Before a brush or a roller can be put away, however, it must be wrapped to protect the bristles or nap. A brush can be returned to its original package or folded in heavy kraft paper, such as a grocery bag, after a final combing to align the bristles, then either hung up or laid flat for storage. A roller should be rolled in heavy kraft paper or placed in a plastic bag—perforated so air circulation will prevent mildew.

After cleaning your equipment, seal up all the containers of paint and thinner and put them away—even small quantities of paint should be saved for future touch-up jobs. To keep air from spoiling the paint, each can must be cleaned around the lip and the lid must be hammered down to make an airtight seal. Paint will keep longest if there is little or no air at all in the container. You can make an air-free container for a small amount of paint by filling a glass jar with the paint (never use a plastic container), then capping the jar tightly; most paints preserved in this way will keep almost indefinitely. Thinners should also be tightly capped to prevent wasteful and potentially dangerous evaporation.

Paints and thinners should be stored out of reach of children and well away from the high temperatures and open flames of such devices as radiators and furnaces. Aerosol cans are particularly

sensitive to heat; if they reach a temperature of 120°F.—which can happen if they are exposed to direct sunlight over a long period of time—they are liable to explode. Water-thinned paints, on the other hand, can be damaged by cold and should be protected from freezing.

The last step in a cleanup is to put the room back in order. First, discard disposable dropcloths and newspapers; if your dropcloths are re-usable, wipe off any large globs of paint and store the cloths with the buckets and trays. As soon as the paint on window frames is dry to the touch, straighten the line of paint that you applied to the panes to make an airtight seal and scrape any drips from the glass (opposite, bottom). Replace light fixtures, switch and outlet covers, hang curtains and blinds and arrange the furniture in the room. Take care to avoid scuffing the newly applied paint; it may not have hardened completely and until it does it will be quite fragile.

Care of Painting Tools

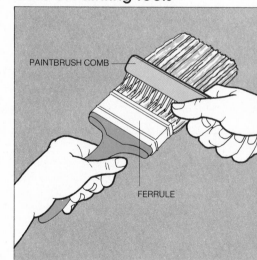

PAINTBRUSH COMB

FERRULE

A comb for a brush. A paintbrush comb loosens stubborn, partially dried paint from the tightly packed bristles just below the ferrule of a brush and also from the spacer plug inside the bristles. The sharp wire teeth of the comb not only penetrate the bristles but also separate them slightly to help the solvent wash away paint residue. At a later stage of the cleanup process, just before the paintbrush is wrapped for storage, draw the comb through the bristles once more to straighten and untangle them. The brush will then be ready for a future paint job.

A spin-drier for brushes and rollers. This ingenious cleanup aid spins off excess solvent or water from paint applicators with a minimum of effort. A brush is secured to the drier by stiff spring clips *(drawing);* alternatively, a roller can be slipped over the clips. When the handle is pushed in and out of the stationary tube, the brush or roller spins at high speed, throwing paint-laden solvent or water from the applicator by centrifugal force. To keep from spraying nearby objects, spin brushes and rollers inside a heavy paper bag or in a garbage can with a plastic liner.

Wrapping a brush. Cut a rectangle of heavy kraft paper—a section of a grocery bag will do—about twice the combined lengths of the ferrule and bristles and about four times the width of the brush. Crease the paper down the center of its longest dimension, place the brush on the paper so that the tips of the bristles are at the crease and roll the brush into the paper *(below)*. Fold the rolled-up paper toward the ferrule along the crease and secure the paper with a rubber band, making a wedge-shaped package that will preserve the taper of the bristles.

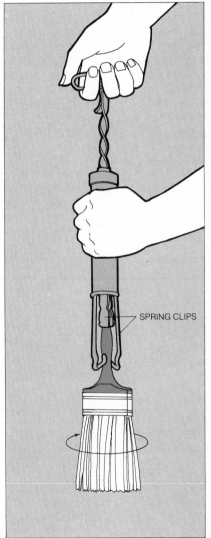

SPRING CLIPS

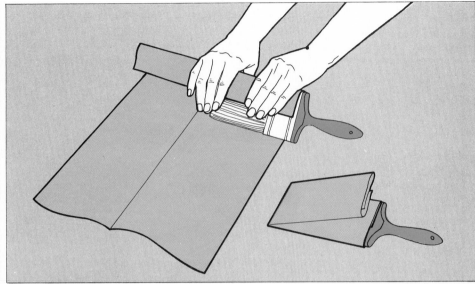

A Neat Edge for Windowpanes

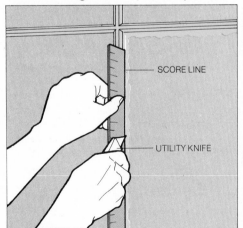

SCORE LINE

UTILITY KNIFE

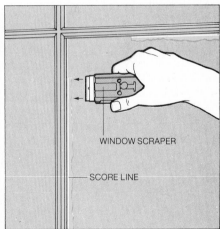

WINDOW SCRAPER

SCORE LINE

1 Scoring the paint. Unless you have used masking tape, you will need to straighten the irregular edges of the paint applied to windowpanes as an airtight seal. For the first step of the job, place the edge of a ruler on a section of glass and against a pane divider or sash. (Shorten the ruler, if necessary, to fit between parts of the window frame.) Score the paint with a utility knife, using the thickness of the ruler as a guide *(drawing)*. Repeat this step for all four edges of each pane.

2 Removing the paint. Lift the irregular edge of the paint from the glass with a window scraper. Position the scraper so that the edge of its blade is parallel to the score line cut by the utility knife, and carefully push the blade under the paint and toward the pane divider, stopping at the score. The paint will come off the glass easily, leaving a neat, straight line.

Unconventional Methods for Unconventional Effects

Once you are familiar with conventional painting techniques, you may want to experiment with the effects that can be achieved by painting graphic designs on a wall—still using regular room paint. Such designs can be used to mask an ungainly structural feature (an awkward angle in the ceiling of an attic room, for instance), enliven an otherwise uninteresting surface *(below, left)*, emphasize a particular piece of furniture *(below, right)* or alter the apparent proportions of a room, making a narrow space seem wider, for example. Any design can be made if you can paint straight lines, circles and arcs. To make perfectly horizontal or vertical straight lines, use a carpenter's level, both to position the line and to serve as a ruler. Then use masking tape to shield the surface of the wall above or below the line.

Several narrow, parallel lines can be painted simultaneously with the aid of a special masking tape ordinarily used for painting stripes on cars. The center portion of this 1-inch-wide tape is scored so that as many as eight $1/16$-inch pull-out strips can be removed; the empty spaces are then easily painted.

Another aid for painting single or double stripes is a striping tool, which comes in a kit that includes one or more bottles for holding the paint, screw caps with wheels that apply the paint and spacers for adjusting the interval between two stripes. The tool is tricky to use, however, so carefully follow the instructions that come with it and test the paint flow on a piece of scrap before using the striper on your wall. Both striping tape and striping tools are available at automobile supply stores.

To draw large circles and arcs, make a simple compass from any thin, narrow strip of wood *(page 48)*. When filling in circles or when painting arcs, try the sign painters' trick of using a baton to steady your hand *(page 49)*.

There are several ways of getting the design onto the surface it is intended for. One way is to draw a small version on paper and make a slide photograph of it, then project the slide on wall or ceiling and trace the enlarged outline. Another is the grid method. With this technique, first mark off on a piece of paper a grid of horizontal and vertical lines 1 inch apart. Add horizontal and vertical coordinates (as on a map) by writing numbers down the sides and letters across the top. Then draw on the grid a rectangle to represent the wall or ceiling in scale, 1 inch on the sketch representing 1 foot of the room measurement. Now chalk a grid on the wall or ceiling with lines 1 foot apart. Label them with coordinates matching those on the paper. Finally, using the coordinates that you have marked on both grids, locate the squares on the wall or the ceiling that correspond to the squares on the sketch, and copy the design in chalk freehand, square by square.

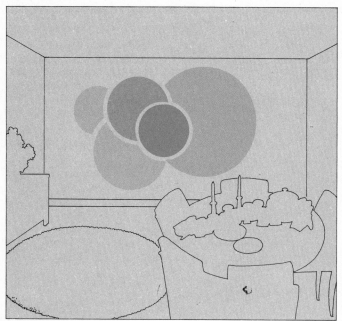

A design using circles. A wall painting is used here to enliven a room. To avoid having to reach over wet paint, start at either side, after chalking the design on the wall grid. Mask all edges of the first circle and paint, using the baton *(page 49)*. Remove the tape when the paint is dry to the touch. Mask and paint adjacent circles across the design. The colors of a design as complex as this should not be garish, especially in a small room; bold, bright colors can be overpowering.

A design using straight and curved lines. This painted headboard, echoing the pattern in the rug at the foot of the bed, sweeps up the wall and across the ceiling to emphasize the bed in a dramatically styled room. To produce a striped design like the one shown here, first transfer the design to the wall and ceiling surfaces, using the grid method explained above, then start by painting the lightest stripe. Next paint the darker stripes on either side of it and continue outward.

Straight Lines

Marking the line. Use a carpenter's level as a ruler, holding it so that the bubble in the tube at the middle of the level is centered for a horizontal line, the bubbles at the ends of the level centered for a vertical line. To extend the line use a chalk line as described on page 108.

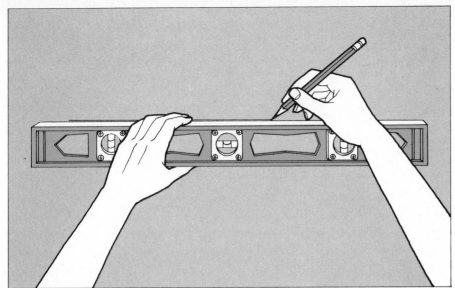

Painting with masking tape. Unless you have an unusually steady hand, place masking tape against your chalk line to ensure clean, even edges. Pull the tape off the reel and affix it to the wall little by little, to keep it straight. If you pull off too much at once, you may get a wavy line. If the tape gets stretched—and wavy—cut it off where it veers from your line and start a fresh piece there. To prevent paint from seeping under the tape, press the edge of the tape firmly with the bowl of a spoon *(drawing)* or the ball of your thumb. After painting, pull the masking tape off gently and smoothly as soon as the paint feels dry to the touch—half an hour for latex paint, several hours for alkyd. If the tape is left on until the paint is completely dry and hard, it may lift up the paint when it is removed.

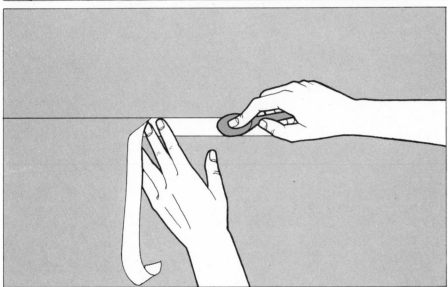

Painting with striping tape. Position striping tape so that as many of the removable strips as necessary align with the lines you want, then remove the desired number of strips *(drawing)*. Because there are so many edges under which paint can seep, be especially diligent in pressing down the edges of the tape along the removed strips. Lightly roughen the exposed area of the wall·with sandpaper for best paint adhesion; even tiny spots where paint fails to adhere will be obvious.

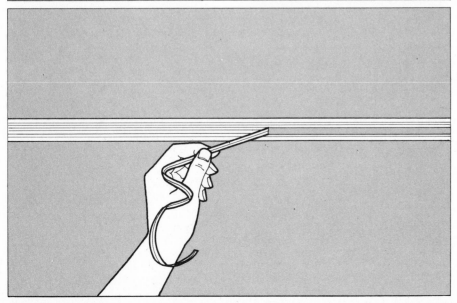

Circles and Arcs

1 **Making the arm of a compass.** A homemade compass for drawing entire circles will also serve for drawing arcs, which are portions of circles. To make the arm of a compass, use a thin strip of wood that is a few inches longer than the radius of the largest circle in your design. Wood ¼ to ½ inch thick and about ½ to 1¼ inches wide is a convenient size. Because the wood is thin, use a small, fine-toothed saw such as a coping saw (drawing) to cut a V-shaped notch as a pencil guide near one end of the strip; the notch holds the pencil tip securely as you draw the circles.

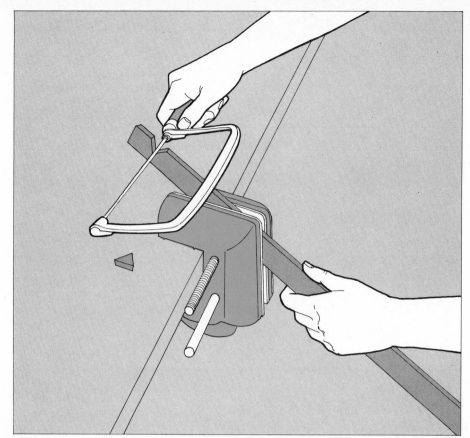

2 **Adding the compass pivot.** Starting at the point of the notch, measure half of the diameter of the desired circle along the compass arm and make a dot at this point. Hammer a thin nail through the dot (drawing) to serve as the pivot on which the compass arm will turn; hammer the nail so only its tip protrudes on the other side of the wood.

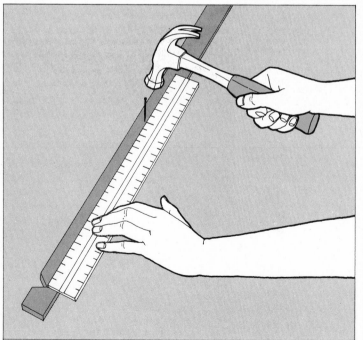

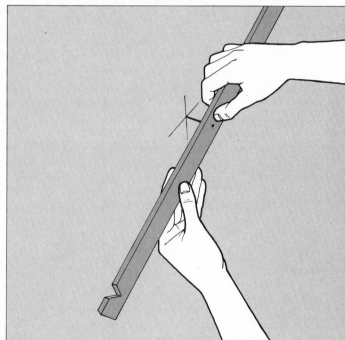

3 **Positioning the compass.** Place the compass arm on the surface to be painted, locating the point of the nail pivot at the center of the circle you wish to draw. Now hammer the nail into the surface, all the way through the compass arm, drawing the arm securely against the surface but not so tightly that the arm cannot turn.

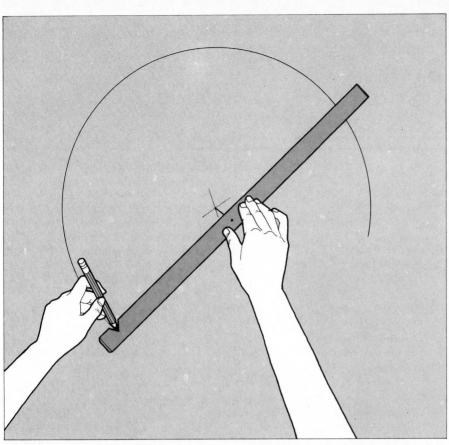

4 **Drawing the circle.** Set the point of a pencil in the point of the notch in the compass arm. Holding the pencil firmly, draw the circle by slowly rotating the compass arm with your other hand.

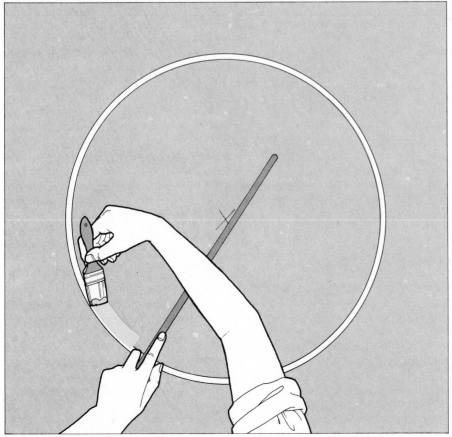

5 **Filling in.** To fill in a circle without getting paint outside the outline, press ¼-inch masking tape around the edge of the circle; the narrow tape will bend without puckering around large circles. Use any strong stick as a painter's baton to support your painting arm; place one end of the baton against the surface being painted and rest your painting arm comfortably upon it, as shown. The same masking tape and baton technique can be used when painting along an arc. If you are sure enough of your hand to paint circles or portions of circles without masking tape, use the beading technique described on page 37.

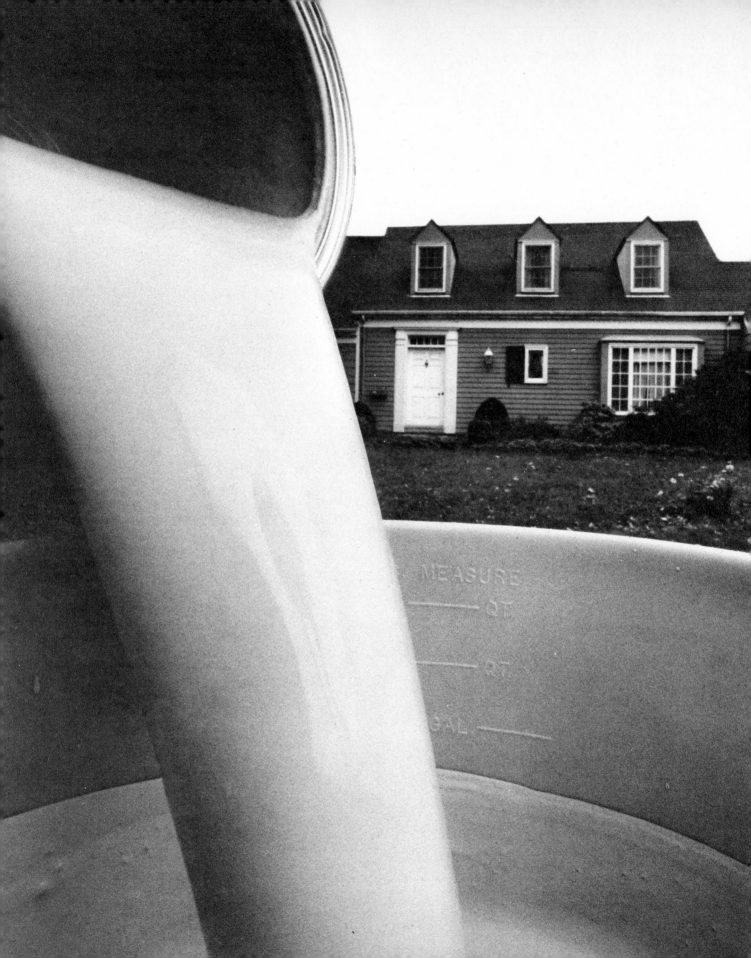

A good start. Paint for the siding on this house pours smoothly from gallon can to bucket, receiving a final mix before it is brushed on. The painter will work from the bucket, recapping the original can to prevent leaves, twigs and other debris from spoiling the paint.

The paint chart on pages 8-9 lists the correct exterior coatings for a wide variety of surfaces; detailed characteristics of these coatings are explained on the following pages. The tools used for painting outdoors are described on pages 54-55.

While you might select an interior paint chiefly to give a face lift to an aging room, you choose an exterior coating not for looks alone but to help protect the outside skin of your house against the elements. The choice also is a bit more complicated because outdoor surfaces are more varied than those inside. They include stucco, cedar shakes, clapboards, aluminum siding and asbestos shingles, as well as cinder block, brick, and hard-to-identify coats of old paint. Despite this range of materials, there is an exterior coating for every surface—and some that work on a great variety of surfaces.

Because exterior paints must adhere to house walls that expand and contract with temperature change, most exterior coatings are more flexible than interior paints from the moment they are applied, and they retain their flexibility longer. To keep the house looking clean and fresh even though it may be bombarded daily with airborne pollutants, alkyd flat exterior paints have a regulated, self-cleaning property called chalking. As a chalking paint dries, white powder forms on its surface. A white pigment called anatase titanium is responsible for this powdering effect, so all chalking paints come in either white or light pastel tones. Once the paint has dried, the anatase titanium produces a chemical reaction that breaks down the resin binder slowly and releases pigment particles in powder form. Although chalking was considered a nuisance at one time because of its tendency to stain brick and even shrubbery below it, manufacturers have developed ways of controlling the chemical reaction carefully: only enough chalk forms to wash away with the average rainfall of temperate areas, carrying dirt with it; none is left to stain adjacent masonry or trim.

Chalking is not necessary for every house, however, and it may even be undesirable in some locations. In regions where rain or snow is heavy, precipitation alone keeps the surface clean. And in dry areas, powdery chalk can build up to dull paint tone and will come off on hands or clothing; in such places a nonchalking latex paint and a yearly washing are the solutions to the dirt problem.

When you decide to paint, it is as important to pick the right weather as it is to pick the right paint. The best temperature range for the job is between 50° and 90° F., since no paint adheres well when it is very hot or very cold. This means that painting should be done in late spring or early fall for most regions in North America. Those seasons are often also rainy, unfortunately. After a heavy rain, wait at least 24 hours before you paint or resume painting; even latex paints, which bond satisfactorily to damp surfaces, will not stick to a wet wall. Check your local weather reports: if rain is forecast, put the job off until all chance of bad weather is past.

A Guide to Exterior Coatings

The same basic kinds of paint are used outside as inside—alkyds, latexes, epoxies and oils. But because outdoor paints must be more elastic and weather resistant than indoor coatings and often must adhere to rougher surfaces, they contain more plasticizers—agents that promote flexibility—and frequently have a higher proportion of resin.

No coating sold for residential use now contains more than a tiny, legally regulated amount of lead, a very hazardous poison that nevertheless once was a major ingredient of paint. Its absence was often blamed by old-time professionals for paint failures, but all authorities agree that the only loss attributable to the removal of lead is some covering power in a few deep colors; the durability and opacity that lead once gave is now provided by synthetic resins and by other pigments.

Even modern paints, however, might cause problems—partially because of the proliferation of types. Latex, the most convenient and versatile, may not adhere when applied over other types. Try to find out what you are painting over —keep a record or ask someone who might know. If you are unable to identify the existing paint layer, your best choice is an alkyd paint, which is least likely to react adversely with an unknown undercoat.

Finishing Paint

All the coatings listed here can be applied with brush, roller or sprayer, unless otherwise indicated. How long a properly applied paint job will last depends largely on when you think it begins to look drab and dull—bright colors fade faster than others, and a clear finish yellows somewhat after a couple of years.

Latex Flat
ODOR FREE
BEST FOR HUMID CONDITIONS

Latex flat is the most popular choice for most exterior siding surfaces because it is thinned and cleaned with water and is the fastest drying. It also allows water va-por to escape through the paint from underneath rather than expanding into a blister. This ability to "breathe" makes latex a good choice for a damp exterior wall. Unlike latex interior paints, exterior latex is often used on raw wood, since the grain exaggeration caused by water solvent is relatively unnoticeable outdoors. Like its interior counterpart, it can also be used on masonry. It does not cover as well as alkyd, however, and if your old surface is still chalking heavily, or is coated with an alkyd finish, latex paint may not adhere perfectly, or, if it holds at first, may not prove quite as durable as an alkyd-base paint.

Alkyd Flat
BEST FOR CHALKING SURFACES

Alkyd exterior paints adhere and cover all surfaces well except unprimed masonry or metal, but special solvents must be used for thinning and cleaning so that they are less convenient to use than latex. On damp surfaces alkyd paint may blister and peel more easily than latex, but alkyd adheres to chalking surfaces better than most water-thinned paints.

Oil Flat
SLOW DRYING

Oil-base flat paints have been outmoded by modern latexes and alkyds: they smell, dry slowly, require mineral spirits or turpentine and are less durable.

Glossy Trim
MORE WASHABLE THAN FLAT

Glossy paints contain more resin than flat ones, giving greater resistance to wear and washing and making them best for windows, doors and shutters. Both alkyd and latex exterior glossy paints wear well and are available in high and semigloss finishes, though latex high gloss is slightly less shiny than its alkyd counterpart. Latex gloss is thinned and cleaned with water and dries faster than alkyd—a big advantage in getting doors and windows back into service. It is also more weather and alkali resistant than alkyd paint. Oil-base trim paint is not as durable as either alkyd or latex, but if used with a zinc-based metal primer it is a good coating for exterior metals such as rain spouts or the undersides of roof gutters.

Marine Paint
VERY DURABLE
EXPENSIVE

These glossy paints are prepared with more epoxy, urethane, acrylic or alkyd resins in proportion to their pigment content than are ordinary exterior finishing paints. This resin step-up increases durability—marine paints were originally designed to protect boats against salt water and bruising weather. Their excellent wearing qualities have made them popular for outdoor wood or metal house trim, although they are expensive.

Porch and Floor Paint
HIGHLY ABRASION RESISTANT
FOR WOOD OR CONCRETE

Formulated to withstand bad weather and traffic on porches and outside steps, these abrasion-resistant alkyd, latex, urethane, rubber-base or epoxy paints are often used indoors also. Rubber-base floor paint gives a flat or semigloss finish and is limited to use on masonry floors. It is water repellent and highly resistant to scrubbing with detergents. Glossy alkyd, urethane and latex types of paint can be used on bare or previously painted wood floors or previously painted masonry floors. Epoxy will coat a smooth, bare floor or any epoxy-coated floor.

Before any floor paint is applied to new concrete, the surface must be carefully prepared to provide "tooth" *(page 14)*. Latex, rubber, urethane or epoxy floor paint can then be applied directly to the concrete. Before an alkyd floor paint is used, however, the surface must be primed *(primers, below)*.

Shingle Paint
POROUS TO LET WOOD BREATHE
A UNIQUE TYPE FOR ASBESTOS

For an opaque finish on asbestos or wood siding shingles, use special flat shingle paints, which permit the escape of moisture that can accumulate behind shingles in damp weather. By allowing shingles to "breathe" as water vapor escapes, these paints help prevent wood rot and paint blisters. Latex, alkyd, or oil-base shingle paints work equally well on bare or most previously coated wood siding shingles. However, asbestos-cement shingles should be coated only with paints labeled for use on them. And wood shingles that are treated with creosote wood preservative should not be painted at all in less than eight years: the oily creosote will prevent the paint from bonding firmly to the wood.

Metal Paint
USED DIRECTLY ON METAL
METALLIC OR COLORFUL FINISH

Metal paints stop rust to greater or lesser degrees and are thinned with mineral-spirit solvents. Aluminum paint (powdered aluminum suspended in oil or alkyd resin) provides a shiny, metallic finish and is particularly durable. It is suitable for most primed metals and is the only paint that will bond to recently creosote-treated wood, providing a surface that usually can be painted over without danger that creosote stains will seep through to mar the finish.

Aluminum paint, however, is not recommended for shingles; it tends to seal in moisture and promote rot.

Glossy oil- or alkyd-base metal paints are available in an assortment of colors and are convenient to use since no primer coat is required. Before applying most of these paints, be sure that you clean the surfaces as you would before applying interior metal primers *(page 17)*.

Some of these oil- or alkyd-base metal paints contain penetrating, rustproofing agents and can be applied directly to rusty metal. Even with these so-called rustproofing paints, however, it is advisable to remove all rust and dirt before applying the coating.

Masonry Paint
LATEX EASIEST TO USE
RUBBER-BASE BEST FOR CINDER BLOCKS

The same types of paint meant for interior masonry also work outside the house: latex, cement paint, rubber-base coatings. In addition, special alkyds can be used on exterior masonry.

Rubber-base paint is the type that is generally recommended for exterior cinder block because the paint is waterproof; it thus prevents moisture from reaching the cinders and causing stains.

If exterior masonry has begun to crumble or if the painted surface is chalking heavily, first use a block filler *(below)* or a clear masonry-sealer *(page 17)*.

Stains and Clear Finishes

The natural materials your house is made of can be displayed yet protected by applying clear or semitransparent finishes rather than pigmented paints. Clear coatings rarely last as long as paint, however, because ultraviolet rays in sunlight penetrate them and alter the character of the surface they cover. This reduces the bond between surface and finish—sometimes in less than two years.

Stains
PROTECTIVE MATTE FINISH
REQUIRE MIXING

Exterior stains, usually used on wood siding and shingles to provide a matte finish, range from nearly transparent to nearly opaque, but all of them contain more pigment than interior stains and so must be mixed like paint before use. The water-base latex stains resist wear and retain their color longer than alkyd or oil-base stains. Latex stains are also more porous and are preferred in damp conditions that might cause an impervious finish to blister. Opaque stains last as long as most pigmented finishing coats.

Varnish
URETHANE TYPE IS TOUGHEST
SPAR VARNISH BEST NEAR SEASHORE

Exterior varnish is used almost exclusively on wood—to protect it from weathering while retaining the natural appearance and color. No exterior varnish lasts as long as an interior one; most have a life expectancy of no more than two years. The most commonly used varnish is spar varnish, which must be renewed every 12 to 16 months, although it provides excellent protection against salt corrosion if kept in good condition. Under most other circumstances, alkyd-base exterior varnish lasts slightly longer than spar varnish. Moisture-cured urethane varnish is the most resistant. An acrylic varnish is designed for ornamental metal.

Primers, Preservatives, Sealers

These special coatings provide raw wood, metal or masonry with extra protection against moisture and rot, and form a bridge when a surface and the desired top coat are incompatible.

Primers
EXTRA FLEXIBLE
A SPECIAL TYPE FOR GALVANIZED STEEL

Exterior primers, which are used under exterior paints, are extra flexible to adjust to wall expansion and contraction. Otherwise, these undercoats are essentially the same as those used inside the house *(page 16)*. A special kind of oil-base primer that contains Portland cement protects exterior steel. Since it has a zinc additive, it can be used on galvanized metal gutters and drains.

Wood Preservative
PROTECTS AGAINST INSECTS AND FUNGI
USED ONLY ON BARE WOOD

Raw wood exterior surfaces can be protected against insect and fungus damage with clear, paintable wood preservatives. Some are also waterproof and will deter warping. The preservatives will not work if the wood has been sealed, stained or painted; any finishing coat can be used over these preservatives.

Creosote, an oily black preservative, is still used because it is inexpensive. But it inhibits adhesion of other coatings for as long as eight years, kills vegetation near it and bleeds through any top coat unless it is first sealed with two coats of aluminum paint.

Block Filler
A MASONRY SEALER
AN UNDERCOAT FOR PAINT

Rough, porous masonry surfaces can be sealed and smoothed by these thick, white coatings that provide a good base for latex, alkyd or oil-base finishes. Block filler can be applied with a paint roller, but a stiff brush is more effective when the surface is rough.

Silicone Water Repellent
A BARRIER TO ALL OTHER COATINGS
PRESERVES APPEARANCE OF WOOD

These nearly invisible coatings reduce to a minimum water seepage through exterior wood surfaces. The silicone repels all topcoats for several years so this preservative should be used only to maintain the original appearance of the wood. Thin and clean up spills with the solvents recommended on the label.

Tool Kit for Exterior Painting

In addition to the standard tools you have on hand, you may need a selection of the specialized tools shown here to paint the outside of your home.

☐ If you face a difficult paint-removing job—a large area or a section with a coating that is hard to get off—the following tools can be helpful: a heavy-duty paint scraper, a power sander, an electric paint remover, and a power drill with a wire-brush attachment. Simpler jobs of paint removal can be done by hand with a wire brush and steel wool, or with sandpaper and putty knives *(pages 21-22)*.

☐ Special tools for making repairs before painting include a cold chisel and mallet for chipping out old caulking or crumbling mortar, a caulking gun for applying new caulking, and a trowel and jointer for laying in new mortar.

☐ Some safety equipment is essential: protective goggles that should be worn when working with power-driven brushes, chisels and corrosive cleaners; and a respirator when working with a power sander or paint sprayer.

☐ A 4-inch flat paintbrush is the standard tool for exterior painting. But a pad applicator may work faster on some broad, flat surfaces; a mitten applicator simplifies the painting of pipes, metal furniture and out-of-the-way places where a brush cannot easily reach; and a rough-surface paintbrush is specifically designed for use on bricks and cinder blocks. (See page 74 for special equipment, generally rented, for spray painting.) The least expensive tool in the kit may be the handiest: an S hook to hang a paint bucket from a rung of an extension ladder.

PAINT SCRAPER

POWER SANDER

WIRE BRUSH

STEEL WOOL

ELECTRIC PAINT REMOVER

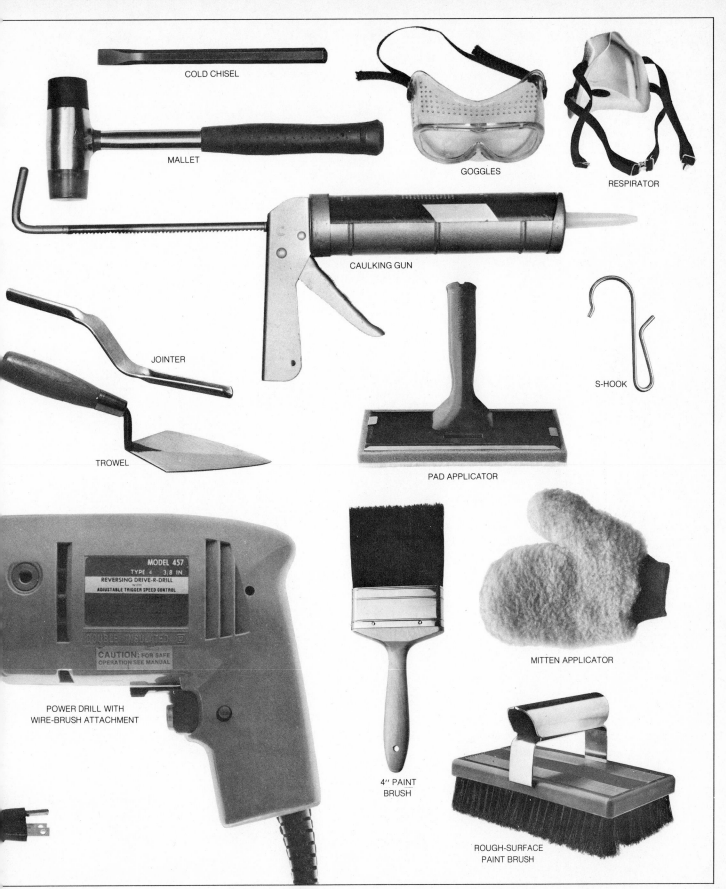

COLD CHISEL

MALLET

GOGGLES

RESPIRATOR

CAULKING GUN

JOINTER

S-HOOK

TROWEL

PAD APPLICATOR

MODEL 457
TYPE 4   3/8 IN
REVERSING DRIVE-R-DRILL
with
ADJUSTABLE TRIGGER SPEED CONTROL

DOUBLE INSULATED

CAUTION: FOR SAFE
OPERATION SEE MANUAL

POWER DRILL WITH
WIRE-BRUSH ATTACHMENT

MITTEN APPLICATOR

4″ PAINT
BRUSH

ROUGH-SURFACE
PAINT BRUSH

Diagnosing Paint Problems

Before you paint the outside of your house, inspect it with the cool, unsparing eye of an appraiser. Wherever you see stains or signs that layers of paint have begun to pull away from the surface, try to identify the cause of the problem and fix it. The damage that you discover is rarely caused by the paint. More often it is the result of a defect such as faulty construction that traps moisture in the outside walls, incomplete surface preparation before the last paint job, incompatible paint, careless painting or a variety of other causes. If you ignore the underlying problem or simply repeat the same mistake when you put on the new paint, the same stains and peeling are likely to recur.

The photographs on these four pages help identify the problems that are most often encountered. All but one of these examples show the exteriors of homes, because paint problems develop more often with exterior coatings that are constantly exposed to changes in temperature than with interior paints. Nevertheless, the information about each problem applies to flaws that occur inside the house as well as out.

As you paint, you may yourself create the two kinds of unattractive paint problems illustrated on this page: blisters and wrinkles. These new-paint problems frequently appear soon after a new coat of paint is applied and should always be corrected immediately.

Blistering. Bubbles pop up when water or solvent vapor is trapped under the paint. Both kinds of blisters are more common with oil and alkyd paints than with water-base coatings. They can be diagnosed by cutting a bubble open. If you see bare wood inside, it is a moisture blister; scrape off the blistered paint, eliminate the source of moisture and let the wood dry thoroughly before repainting. If you see paint inside the bubble, it is a solvent blister caused by painting in the heat of direct sunlight, which dries the surface of the paint too quickly, forming a skin that traps solvent. Sand smooth and repaint.

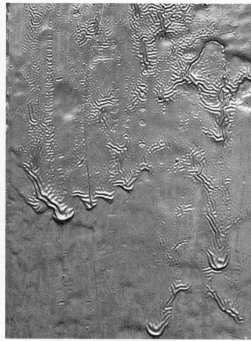

Wrinkling. Unsightly convolutions occur when oil or alkyd paints are applied too thick. At first a film forms quickly and smoothly across the surface. But as the excess paint under the film dries, it decreases in volume; the film cannot shrink enough to fit tautly, and droops down into wrinkles. To get rid of wrinkles, sand them smooth and repaint with a thinner coat.

Peeling from wood. Paint curls away from surfaces like the window frame at right because the coating was applied over dirt, grease or loose paint, or because the wood contained moisture. Before repainting a peeled surface, remove all loose paint *(page 65)*, eliminate the source of dampness if possible and let the wood dry thoroughly. If you cannot prevent the wood from becoming damp because moisture is seeping through from inside the house or because of drainage problems, try repainting the stripped wood with thin coatings of latex primer and paint. They are more porous than oil or alkyd coatings and usually allow water vapor to pass through.

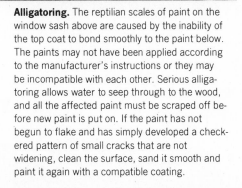

Alligatoring. The reptilian scales of paint on the window sash above are caused by the inability of the top coat to bond smoothly to the paint below. The paints may not have been applied according to the manufacturer's instructions or they may be incompatible with each other. Serious alligatoring allows water to seep through to the wood, and all the affected paint must be scraped off before new paint is put on. If the paint has not begun to flake and has simply developed a checkered pattern of small cracks that are not widening, clean the surface, sand it smooth and paint it again with a compatible coating.

Peeling from masonry. Paint flakes from stucco, concrete and brick not only for the same reasons that it peels from wood, but also because of chemical compounds called alkalis, found in most masonry, which destroy paint adhesion. Extensive peeling can best be remedied by having all old paint removed by sandblasting. To prevent peeling, seal the masonry with sealer *(page 8)* and paint it with an alkali-resistant coating.

Efflorescence peeling. The paint on the brick wall at right is disintegrating because of efflorescence, which can also affect concrete and other masonry. It arises when alkali compounds in the masonry are dissolved by moisture and carried to the surface. When the water evaporates, the compounds crystalize under the paint, pushing it away from the wall. If efflorescence becomes a problem on older masonry near pipes, gutters or downspouts, check for leaks. Follow the instructions on page 69 to remove the deposits.

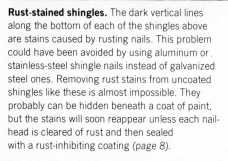

Rust-stained shingles. The dark vertical lines along the bottom of each of the shingles above are stains caused by rusting nails. This problem could have been avoided by using aluminum or stainless-steel shingle nails instead of galvanized steel ones. Removing rust stains from uncoated shingles like these is almost impossible. They probably can be hidden beneath a coat of paint, but the stains will soon reappear unless each nailhead is cleared of rust and then sealed with a rust-inhibiting coating (*page 8*).

Rusted metal. The old steel gutters above are studded along the upper edge with rust pits that started when the paint deteriorated enough to let water through, probably because of inadequate preparation or neglect. Rust washing down from the pits has caused broad, vertical stains on the lower part of the gutter. These gutters should be replaced with more durable aluminum or plastic ones. Less extensive rust on steel can be arrested and painted over as described on page 66.

Chalk stains. The brick wall at right has been discolored by paint chalk that has washed down from the siding above it. Chalking paint helps keep the siding clean, but should not be used where the chalk can streak areas below. The only remedy for this situation is to wash the siding and repaint it with a nonchalking paint. The brick can be restored by scrubbing with detergent.

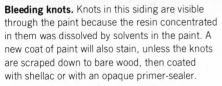

Bleeding knots. Knots in this siding are visible through the paint because the resin concentrated in them was dissolved by solvents in the paint. A new coat of paint will also stain, unless the knots are scraped down to bare wood, then coated with shellac or with an opaque primer-sealer.

Mildew. The dark discoloration near the porch of this house is caused by mildew fungus growing on the paint. These unsightly molds trap airborne dirt, and some varieties can eat through the paint. There is no lasting prevention for mildew; it will grow wherever conditions are right—usually in damp, shady areas. Mildew patches should be killed with a fungicide such as chlorine bleach (*page 63*) before a house is repainted or fungus will grow through the new coat or cause it to peel.

Estimating the Paint You Will Need

The amount of paint needed for the outside of a house is calculated in much the same way as for a room *(page 13)*. The perimeter of the house multiplied by its height gives the total outside area. If you are using a different coating for trim, subtract from this figure the area of doors (approximately 21 square feet each) and window frames (approximately 15 square feet each for the average size). Then divide the resulting figure by the number of square feet one gallon of your paint will cover. The result will be the total paint requirement for one coat if you are using conventional brushes, rollers or exterior shingle pads; if you plan to use a sprayer *(pages 74-75)*, you may have to double the size of your paint order since the sprayer applies the equivalent of two coats of paint at once. Remember as you figure

out how much paint to buy that the coverage figures printed on the paint-can label may be optimistic.

You will need a helper to measure the perimeter of your house. Use a ball of twine tied to a stake or a steel tape and have the helper steady one end as you both move around the house. Or run a ball of string all around the outside—again with your helper to keep the line in place—and then measure the length of the string.

To figure the height of your house, climb a ladder to the eaves, drop a weighted string to the ground and measure the length. For a rough estimate, figure 10 feet for each story and add 2 feet if your house has gables. Or count the number of courses of clapboards and shingles and multiply by the height of a single course.

To estimate the amount of outside trim paint needed, measure one shutter or door (or one of each size if they vary) and multiply that area by the number of shutters or doors on your house. Then add about 15 square feet for the trim on each window. If you intend to paint gutters or edging, assume that each foot of length includes a square foot of area: for example, if you have 60 feet of metal gutter along your eaves, buy enough trim paint to cover 60 square feet.

If making all these trim calculations is inconvenient, however, the rule of thumb is to buy one gallon of trim paint for every six gallons of paint you buy for the siding. That should cover most needs—unless you have lots of shutters and more than the usual two or three outside doors.

Estimating the Time It Will Take

You can paint the outside of an average house with a brush or roller in a week—or less—if the weather is fair. Small houses will take less time, larger ones a day or so more. Spraying cuts time on any house down to as little as a day. To calculate how long it will take to paint your house with a brush or roller, count on covering 120 square feet an hour on a smooth nonporous surface, and about 100 square feet of raw wood or 60 square feet of rough masonry or shingles per hour. Preparations take longer outside than in: do major repairs well in advance. Then, after calculating the time you need for actual painting, add on one third more hours for the final preparation, such as masking fixtures and shrubbery. Double the time if you must make heavy repairs as part of the painting job itself.

Your own endurance is also a factor in making a time estimate. You cannot work as fast as the contractor who once painted your house in a day or two. He was used to the work, and he may have had an assistant. Get a helper yourself.

One of you can cover siding while the other trims. The gain in efficiency is so great that you may be able to cut job time by as much as two thirds.

Your outdoor work time is also subject to seasonal change. The long days of late spring and early fall expand your work hours, and paint will dry quickly in the sunny warmth of these months. You should not paint in direct sunlight, however, for your own comfort and to prevent paint from drying so fast that you drag your brush over a drying coat. Your schedule depends on the sun for another reason: it is your guide to the place to start working. Observe where the sun hits the house in early morning. See where it moves as the day progresses. Then, when you are ready to paint, start on the side just abandoned by the sunlight and follow the sun around the house. Note the comments on page 78 about temperature.

With more than one coat, paint drying time will be important in your planning. The table below lists the average times in which several coatings

harden enough for a second coat on a surface such as prepainted clapboard. The drying times for latex also hold true when it is used on smooth, dry masonry, but latex may take up to 50 per cent longer to dry if it is applied to a damp surface. If you are painting on a very porous surface such as bare wood, cut the drying time about 20 per cent.

Alkyd flat house paint, 24 hours
Latex flat house paint, 2-4 hours
Alkyd glossy house paint, 12-48 hours
Latex glossy house paint, 4 hours
Alkyd trim paint, 12 hours
Latex trim paint, 4 hours
Alkyd metal paint, 12 hours
Oil metal paint, 2-4 days
Latex masonry paint, 4-12 hours
Alkyd primer, 24 hours
Latex primer, 2 hours
Zinc-rich metal primer, 24 hours
Opaque exterior stain, 8-10 hours
Semitransparent stain, 6-8 hours (interior) and 8-10 hours (exterior)
Silicone water repellent, 2-3 hours
Wood sealer, 2 hours

Before You Paint: Preparing Exterior Surfaces

Getting the outside of your home ready for a new coat of paint is essential because it makes the paint job not only look better but last longer. Even though outside paints are tougher than those made for inside use, they must have clean, solid and dry surfaces to bond to.

Most homes need no more than a hosing to remove minor accumulations of dirt. And small areas of deeply embedded grime can be cleaned with detergent. But your house probably has a wide variety of surfaces that may require special attention to get them ready for paint. The drawings and instructions on this and the following pages will help you assess what needs to be done and guide you in doing the job right.

If large areas on the outside of your house are dirty, consider renting a high-pressure water cleaning device (pages 62-63), which does the work fast and removes not only dirt but peeling and loose paint as well.

Patches of mildew can also be cleared off the house by adding a household bleach to the power spray's water supply or by following the directions on page 63. Rust and other metal stains repel most paints so these deposits must be removed and prevented from recurring. If the stains are caused by leaks, stop them at the source: seal joints (see page 68 for caulking instructions), fix broken downspouts and gutters and repair damaged roofs. The steel nails in clapboard or shingle siding are a common source of rust streaks; scrape them and seal them from moisture (below) so that the problem will not recur. If screens or gutters are depositing metal stains on paint, scrape the metal clean with a wire brush and then paint it. Copper screens can be sealed with clear acrylic varnish.

If any of the old paint is damaged or loose—examples of typical deterioration are illustrated on pages 56-59—it must come off. Use hand sanders and scrapers (pages 21-22) to remove small patches from clapboard siding. Chemical paint removers (page 22) are efficient, especially around window trim and moldings, where it may be difficult to probe with a tool. While you are working on wood surfaces, seal any knots and oozing sap pores with shellac (page 29).

Peeling paint on metal and masonry surfaces usually comes off easily with a wire brush, although stubborn cases may have to be sand-blasted by a professional. Chemical paint removers usually work well on metals, but seldom work satisfactorily on brick. After you remove the paint you may have to follow some of the special procedures that are described on pages 64 and 66 to give the metal or masonry surface enough "tooth" to hold a coat of paint.

More than routine cleaning and paint scraping may be required before you start painting if you have not kept up with some basic outdoor maintenance tasks such as replacing split shingles, loose caulking around windows and doors, and loose mortar in brick walls. These three jobs (pages 67-69) cannot be left till later because the repair will then mar your new paint job.

Eliminating rust stains. Use sandpaper or steel wool to take off stains caused by rusted nailheads. Clean the nailhead itself with the same material until bright metal appears. If you are working on clapboard or any other smooth wood, drive the nail ⅛ inch below the surface with a hammer and nail set (page 30). Cover the nailhead with a rust-inhibiting metal primer. When it dries, fill the nail hole with putty or spackle; give this filler a chance to dry and then coat it and any bare wood with a primer. Flathead nails, which cannot be countersunk, should simply be sandpapered bright and coated with a primer.

If rust has worked its way into wood, as nailhead stains on textured shingles do, removing the stain would remove too much wood. The only remedy for this problem is to scrape and seal the nailhead, and then stain the shingle with an opaque stain, or paint it to hide the rust.

High-powered House Cleaning

A high-pressure spray cleaning device considerably reduces the labor of removing dirt, mildew, sea-spray salt, paint-chalk accumulations, or even peeling paint. A medium-sized one-story house can be cleaned in about two hours.

A typical spray cleaner takes water from the supply system of the house and pumps it out in a narrow jet at a pressure of 600 pounds per square inch to blast off dirt and loose paint. It can also pump water from a barrel if necessary. Household liquid detergents or chemical cleaners, stored in the container on top of the pump housing, can be mixed with the water for more efficient cleaning when needed. Electricity from a regular house receptacle powers the pump and also heats the water to 140° F.

Spray cleaners can be rented from many paint and hardware stores. Wear goggles when spraying with detergent or chemical solutions. And always ground the electrical connections *(below)* to prevent possible electric shock.

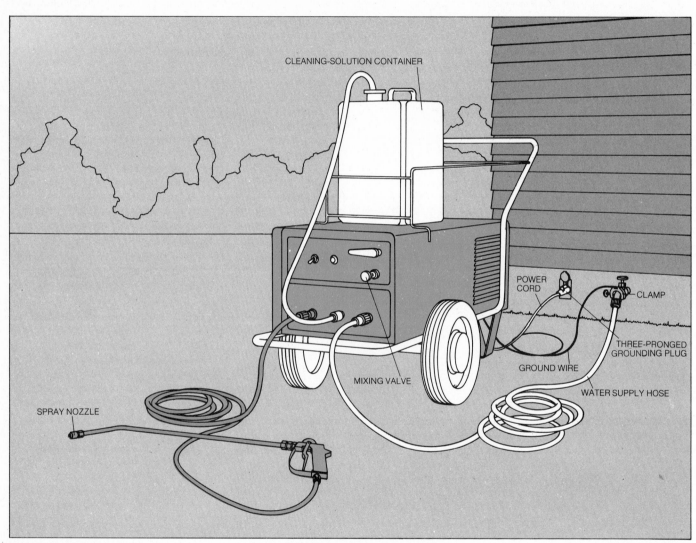

CLEANING-SOLUTION CONTAINER

POWER CORD

CLAMP

THREE-PRONGED GROUNDING PLUG

GROUND WIRE

WATER SUPPLY HOSE

MIXING VALVE

SPRAY NOZZLE

1 **Making the connections.** An ordinary ¾-inch garden hose connects the spray cleaner to an outside water faucet or to a barrel. A smaller hose, furnished with the unit, couples the cleaning-solution container—on top of the unit—to the pump. A third hose, also part of the equipment, carries water and cleaning solution under high pressure from the pump to the nozzle.

The flow of cleaning solution is controlled by a valve on the unit. Because powder granules may damage pump seals, use only heavy-duty liquid detergents for routine cleaning or full-strength liquid chlorine bleach to remove mildew. The control valve can be adjusted to secure the desired dilution of cleaner in the jet spray.

Two separate electrical connections are needed to run the cleaner and to provide double grounding for safety. The unit's heavy-duty electrical power cord must be plugged into a receptacle that will accept a three-pronged plug. Removing the grounding prong or plugging the unit into an ungrounded receptacle is dangerous. The unit's second electrical connection, a thin grounding wire, must be clamped to a cold-water pipe.

2 **Spraying on the cleaner.** After making the necessary liquid and electrical connections, fill the cleaning-solution container and set the valve on the unit to mix the cleaning solution with the water supply. Turn on the heating element also if the walls are very grimy. Hold the nozzle about 2 feet away from the wall (*left*) and point it straight at the surface. Squeeze the trigger to start the spray and begin at the top of a section, sweeping back and forth in 6-to-8-foot strokes. Continue to work downward for about 10 minutes so the solution will penetrate and loosen dirt and stains.

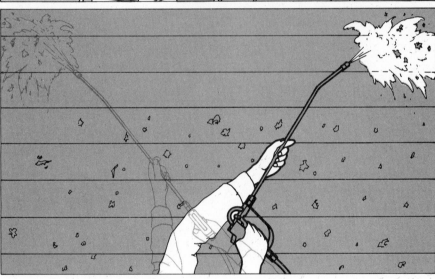

3 **Rinsing off.** To flush dirt and detergents from a wall, and to blast off loose paint, set the valve to water only. Start at the top of a section and hold the nozzle about 6 inches away from the surface. Point it at a 45° angle to the wall in the direction you are moving the nozzle so that the full force of the jet shears off any loose paint chips. At the end of each sweep, reverse the direction in which you point the nozzle but keep it at a 45° angle.

Doing Away with Mildew

Mildew, a fungus that can feed on oil-base paints, thrives on damp and shaded walls. Since it prevents any new paint from adhering, it must be completely removed. Scrubbing alone is not sufficient to prevent regrowth, however. Mildew spores embedded in the surface must be killed.

The first step is to test dirty stains that look like the mildew shown on page 59. Apply full-strength liquid chlorine laundry bleach to a suspected area with a rag. If the discoloration disappears in a few moments, it is mildew. To remove it, make a cleaning solution of one cup of chlorine laundry bleach to one gallon of warm water. You can also make the solution with one cup of an alkali detergent, such as TSP if it is available in your community, or a combination of one-half cup of each. Any of these formulas will kill mildew.

Make sure any loose paint has been removed. Then vigorously scrub the solution on the mildewed area with a stiff-bristled brush or spray it on with a high-pressure jet until all the mildew disappears. Flush the surface thoroughly with clean water and let the section dry thoroughly before painting. If you are applying an oil-base paint, add a mildew-inhibiting agent (available at paint stores) to the primer coat. Additives are not necessary for water-base paints because they do not contain oil for the fungus to feed on.

Treatments for Concrete

Patios, garages, driveways and basements must be thoroughly cleaned and dried before painting, for no paint will adhere to masonry surfaces that are slick with grease or oil. Scrubbing with hot water and detergent, such as TSP *(page 20)*, will remove most stains caused by vegetable oil or animal fat.

Basements, garages, floors and driveways, however, are likely to have heavy deposits of petroleum-based grease and oil and you will need a specially formulated concrete cleaner to get rid of them. Commonly known as degreasers, these cleaners are sold in powdered, liquid and aerosol form. The inexpensive powdered type is spread over the stain and then moistened; the liquid type is used undiluted. With both types, the surface has to be scrubbed vigorously with a broom or brush. The mixture is left in place for the time specified on the label, then hosed off. An aerosol degreaser is the most expensive of the three types, but it is also the easiest to use *(right)*; only stubborn spots need scrubbing.

Before concrete is painted for the first time, it should be etched with muriatic acid to neutralize the alkali in the concrete and roughen the surface to help the paint adhere. (Follow the directions given at right.)

When existing paint on a concrete surface is in bad condition, or is a much darker shade than you want, you should consider removing it before you repaint. To do so, apply a solution of one pound of lye to five pints of water with a scrub brush. After the paint comes off, flush the surface thoroughly and etch the surface with muriatic acid, flush it again and let it dry completely. Caution: Muriatic acid and lye are powerful, corrosive chemicals; wear heavy rubber gloves, goggles and protective clothing when you are working with them, and do not let the solutions spill onto any surface except the concrete itself.

Concrete block and cinder block can be treated by the methods described above, but their surfaces are porous and do not hold paint well. You can create a smoother surface by priming with a coat or two of block filler *(page 53)*.

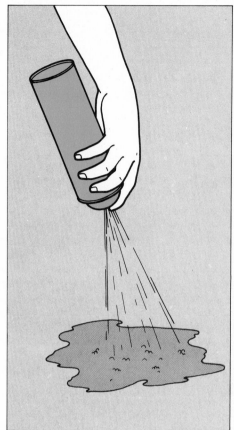

Using a degreaser. The easiest way to remove oil from concrete surfaces is with an aerosol degreaser. Use a degreaser specifically labeled as safe for asphalt if you are working close to an asphalt surface. Simply spray the stained spot liberally *(above)* and let the degreaser stand for the time recommended by the manufacturer. Caution: Vapors from these cleaners are flammable and toxic; do not smoke while using them, extinguish all fires and open all doors and windows if you are working in an enclosed area. After the degreaser has dissolved the oil stains, hose the residue off if there is a drain nearby. If there is no drain use a mop and bucket, since grass or plants can be damaged by the chemical degreaser even if it is diluted by rinse water. Let the surface dry completely before painting.

Etching concrete. To prepare bare concrete surfaces for paint, make an etching solution of one part concentrated muriatic acid with five parts water. Caution: Always pour acid into water, never water into acid. A gallon of this solution will cover about 100 square feet of concrete. Wearing heavy rubber gloves, apply the acid solution to the concrete with a long-handled scrub brush *(above)*. When the solution stops bubbling on the concrete surface, flush it off into a drain or mop it up. Let the concrete dry. If small patches do not dry readily, repeat the flushing procedure.

Removing Paint from Clapboard

If you have large areas of loose or peeling paint on clapboard, or places where layers of paint have built up an overthick coating, you will need something faster than a putty knife or a sanding block to get the paint off. Try the rigid-blade scraper or the power sander shown below, which can be rented from paint stores. Do not use a disk sanding attachment on a power drill; it leaves circular scratches that will show through paint. An orbital sander, which vibrates in a narrow radius, avoids such scratches. A belt sander also serves, but is hard to control and can damage wood.

Heat is an efficient paint remover for oil-base and alkyd paints, if just enough is applied to melt the paint and not burn the wood. Use an electric paint remover *(bottom)*, which is a heating coil mounted inside a protective shield. Do not use a propane torch; it can scorch wood and set a house afire. Take latex paints off with chemical removers or by sanding.

Scraping paint off. A rigid, hook-shaped replaceable blade makes this scraper a more efficient tool for removing paint from wood than a flexible-blade putty knife. The scraper will damage wood, however, if it is pulled across the grain with too much force; work carefully until you find the minimum pressure needed to take the paint off.

Sanding paint off. The most efficient power tool for clearing away large areas of damaged paint from clapboard is an orbital sander. Keep the sanding surface flat against the clapboard as you work, and keep the tool moving to avoid oversanding any spots. Caution: Always wear a respirator when you are using a power sander.

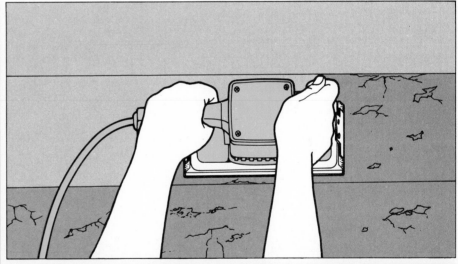

Lifting paint off with heat. Heavy deposits of paint can often be removed more quickly by heat than by sanding. Set the heating element of the paint remover over the painted surface. When the paint begins to sizzle, pull the remover firmly across the heated area, scraping the paint off as you go; keep a putty knife in your other hand to scrape off any paint that remains on the area, and to clean the device itself. Use the heating device with caution: do not touch the heating element, and wear gloves and heavy clothing to protect yourself from hot scraps of paint.

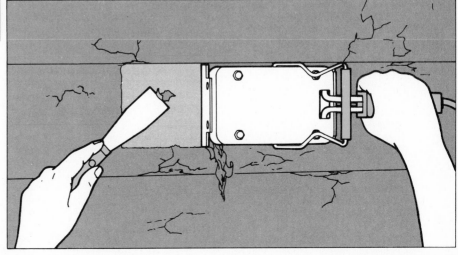

Brushing and Polishing Metal

Paint adheres best to metal when the surface is bright and bare, with all traces of finish and corrosion removed, but you can usually get a satisfactory bond by wire-brushing off loose or damaged paint and rust and painting over the sections where old paint still adheres firmly.

Wear protective goggles to keep grit out of your eyes. To prepare steel surfaces, scrape the paint and rust off by hand with a stiff wire brush, or with a wire-brush attachment in a power drill.

Prepare aluminum surfaces by wire-brushing off loose paint; then clean the metal areas with a commercial cleaning solution specifically made for aluminum. Both steel and aluminum should be given an undercoat of a zinc-base metal primer paint *(page 17)*.

To prepare ornamental brass fixtures —doorknobs, knockers—for a fresh protective coating, remove all remaining traces of previous coatings with lacquer remover and clean off tarnish with brass polish and a soft rag. Do not use steel wool or a wire brush; either will destroy the mirror-like surface of the brass. Then apply clear lacquer from an aerosol can or brush on polyurethane varnish.

Stripping metal by hand. Peeling paint and minor rust spots are easily removed from wrought-iron guard rails and outdoor furniture with a stiff wire brush. If the surfaces are badly rusted, do not try to get down to bright metal; just take off flakes and soft spots and brush off all powdered rust. To prevent rust buildup in the future, apply two undercoats of oil- or alkyd-base primer containing zinc *(page 17)*. Let the first primer coat dry thoroughly before applying the second.

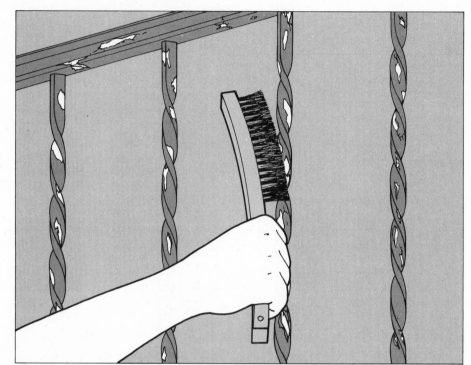

Fast stripping with a power brush. A wire brush attached to a power drill will shorten any metal cleaning task, and it is almost a necessity for such jobs as stripping down steel gutters and downspouts or taking peeling paint off large areas of aluminum. A cup-shaped brush, shown at right, covers a large area quickly. For tight spaces, such as the insides of a narrow gutter or a series of grooves, use the narrow-edged type shown in the inset. Make sure that you wear goggles and gloves when using either type of brush, and always keep the drill pointed away from you; if you tip the edge of the brush toward you, it may drive the grit straight at you.

Replacing Broken Shingles

Replace all broken or warped shingles before you refinish them. Painting over bad shingles may disguise the damage, but it will permit water to seep behind the good shingles and cause further deterioration. The steps for replacing asbestos and wood shingles are basically similar, but asbestos shingles are more fragile and require extra care. For example, nails cannot be driven through asbestos shingles; holes for nails must be drilled in them instead.

Before painting or staining shingles, be sure the surfaces are clean. Small patches of dirt can be washed off by hand with a rag, and bits of loose paint scraped off with a wire brush. But if the whole house needs a thorough going-over, doing the job with a high-pressure spray cleaner, described on pages 62-63, saves time and effort.

Asbestos Shingles

1 Removing a shingle. Break up the damaged shingle with a hammer, taking care not to damage sound shingles around it—asbestos shingles are fragile. Slip a hacksaw blade under the course above the broken shingle, and saw off the nails that held it in place. Wear a glove to protect your hand. Remove all broken shingles.

2 Installing the new shingle. Slip the shingle under the upper course and hold it in place. Drill two new nail holes through the new shingle just below the bottom edge of the upper course, using a power drill with a carbide bit. The new shingle can then be nailed in place, using nonrusting galvanized or aluminum nails.

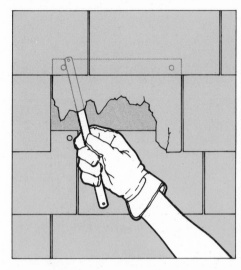

Wood Shingles

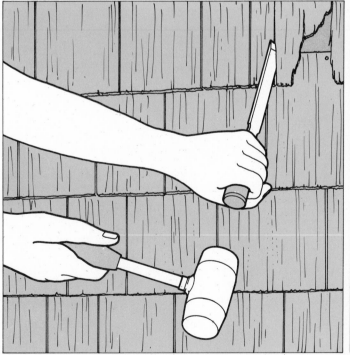

1 Removing a shingle. Split the shingle with a wood chisel along the grain, breaking it into narrow strips and slivers of wood. Cut the nails under the upper course with a hacksaw blade, following the method for asbestos shingles (above), and pull out all the pieces of old shingle.

2 Installing the new shingle. Slip the shingle under the upper course and hold it in place. Drive two or three galvanized or aluminum nails through the new shingle just below the bottom edge of the course above it. It is not necessary to drill nail holes through wood shingles first.

Resealing Joints

Crumbling caulking along doors, windows, corners and roofs makes a bad base for new paint. Even if the paint adheres to it, moisture will seep past it and cause blisters and peeling later on. It should be replaced. Two types of caulking are now available: plastic caulking, which lasts as long as 10 years but requires tedious preliminaries to application, and oil-base caulking, which is less expensive and easier to work with but considerably less durable.

Butyl or vinyl plastic caulking must be put down on bare surfaces. To get adhesion between the new caulking and bare wood or brick, all the old caulking in a damaged joint must be chiseled out *(top right)*. If you must save the time such preparation requires—there may be a lot of caulking to replace—use oil-base caulking. Remove only loose pieces and apply the new caulking directly over the old caulking that is still sound.

Both kinds of caulking are sold in throwaway cartridges for use with an inexpensive caulking gun *(center)*. Work only when joints are dry and the temperature is above 50° F.; caulking will not stick to damp or cold surfaces.

1 Removing old caulking. Wherever you see missing or deteriorated caulking, clean loose pieces out of the joint with a screwdriver or knife. If you are using oil-base caulking, reseal the section as shown in Step 3 below. But to apply long-lasting butyl or vinyl compound, you must take out of the affected section all old caulking that is still sticking to the joint; use a cold chisel and mallet, then dust with a rag or brush. Caution: wear goggles to protect your eyes from chips.

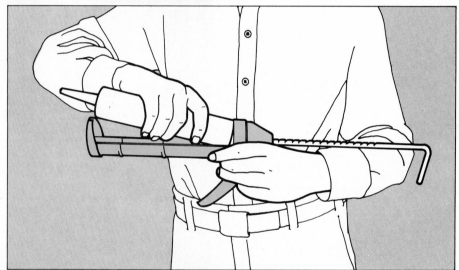

2 Loading the caulking gun. To load a gun with a cartridge of caulking—either plastic or oil-base —turn the plunger rod until its teeth face up, then pull the rod back as far as it will go. Slip the cartridge into the gun and turn the rod so the teeth face down. Snip the plastic spout of the cartridge to make an opening about ¼ inch wide.

3 Applying caulking. Set the spout into the joint and squeeze the trigger gently until the caulking begins to flow; then pull the spout steadily along the joint while squeezing just enough to fill but not overflow the joint. The caulking strip should have a slightly concave shape.

Cleaning and Restoring Brick

Three different problems may be encountered in preparing brickwork for a new coat of paint: flaking patches of old paint, the whitish powder or powdery crust called efflorescence *(page 58)*, and crumbling mortar. An ordinary wire brush will take off loose paint, but the other ailments require more extensive treatments.

Efflorescence must be dissolved with an acid solution, the solution neutralized with an alkali, and the entire wall flushed with clean water. Follow this sequence of steps: Scrub the crust of efflorescence off the bricks with a solution made with one part of muriatic acid and 10 parts of water. Caution: Always pour acid into water, never water into acid. If the deposits do not come off easily, make the solution stronger—one part acid to eight parts water. After the masonry is clean, scrub with a solution of one part ammonia to two parts water to neutralize the acid. Then flush with a hose, working down from the top of the wall.

Both solutions used for this job are corrosive. Wear goggles and gloves, and use a long-handled scrub brush. And make sure you flush directly into a drain.

Chiseling out damaged mortar and laying in new, called tuck pointing, calls for some of the skills of a mason—but the skills are easy to master, and the work, though time consuming, is not difficult. You will need special tools such as a trowel and mortarboard to apply the mortar, and a jointer to firm and shape the mortar in place. The tip of the trowel can be used for this step, but the jointer gives a tighter seal and an even shape.

After cleaning and pointing the brickwork, let the bricks and mortar dry for several days. For best results on bare bricks, apply an undercoat of primer *(pages 52-53)*; otherwise the porosity of the bricks may absorb paint unevenly, giving a mottled appearance.

Tuck Pointing

1 Taking out broken mortar. Remove loose and crumbling mortar from between bricks by chipping it out with a cold chisel and mallet. Take out enough mortar so that bare brick is exposed on at least one side of every joint you repair; the new mortar must have brick to adhere to. Chip deeply into the joint as well; it is better to take out some solid mortar than to leave any broken pieces behind. Clean the dust from the joint with a brush. Caution: Wear goggles during this procedure.

2 Laying in fresh mortar. Prepare a small batch of mortar. Use packaged mortar, available at building-supply stores, or prepare your own by combining one part portland cement with three parts fine sand and enough water to make a fairly stiff mixture—one that does not run down the wall. Dampen the bricks inside the empty joint with a brush. (Do not use a hose; you may force water behind the bricks and damage the wall.) Press mortar firmly into the joint with a trowel. Use a small board to hold the mortar, or a handy "hawk" with a handle underneath.

3 Shaping the joint. Use a mason's tool called a jointer, or striker, to force the still-wet mortar between the bricks, and to give a smooth, even finish to the surface. After the mortar has dried —three or four days—neutralize its alkali, which can damage paint: brush on a solution of one pound of zinc sulfate crystals to a quart of water. Gloves and goggles should be worn when you are working with this caustic solution.

Painting a House in Logical Order

Painting the exterior of a house calls for the same top-to-bottom strategy—as well as many of the same basic tools and techniques—as painting the interior. There are differences, of course. Scale is one. Painting the upper reaches of a house exterior is more perilous than any indoor job. And the variety of exterior construction details means that the painting sequence requires careful planning. There are also methods for applying paint, described on the following pages, that are more useful outdoors than in.

The safe ways to paint from extension ladders are described on pages 10-12. Many houses have dormers, however, that can be painted only from a sloping roof. Use a ladder that reaches at least 3 feet above the edge. This enables you to step safely from the ladder onto the roof without standing on the top two rungs or climbing over the eaves. On the roof be extra cautious: wear shoes with non-slip soles, use a ladder and ladder hook *(page 12)* for foot- and handholds, and sit down as much as possible.

An exterior paint job has two major stages: first coating the sides of the house and then the trim. Start on the side that is not in direct sunlight *(page 60)*. If there are dormers on that side, paint them first, leaving the overhang, trim and windows for the next stage. Then continue down to the main section. Paint the siding in horizontal strips, moving the ladder as necessary to work safely. (If you paint in vertical strips, you will have to adjust the length of the ladder oftener.)

When the siding is complete, start on the trim. Again, begin with the dormers, then do overhangs, gutters and downspouts as you come to them. Next, do the windows, shutters and doors of the main part of the house. Door and window exteriors are painted the same way as their inside surfaces *(pages 41-42)*.

After painting the trim, do the porch railings, then the stairs and foundation. If stairs must be used before they have a chance to dry, paint all the risers but only alternate treads, and then do the rest after the first half has dried. The final flourish is a coat of tough urethane varnish on wooden thresholds.

SIDING

TRIM

RAILINGS

PORCHES AND FOUNDATION

The sequence of painting. This drawing shows most features that must be painted in a typical two-story house. Color (see key) is used here not to suggest a decoration scheme but as a guide to the order, top to bottom in each case, in which elements of the house should be painted.

Special Methods for the Outside

The basic tools for exterior house painting are the same kinds of brushes and rollers that are used indoors, with a few variations on how they are handled. For instance, there is a special technique, shown at right, for painting clapboard siding; the same technique can be easily adapted to painting shingles.

Be prepared for tiring work. The large, heavy 4-inch brush frequently used for painting outdoor surfaces, the side-to-side arm motions and the extensive area to be covered will inevitably result in fatigue, and there is no way of holding the brush that will avoid that problem. So grip the paintbrush like a tennis racquet, or flex your fingers on the ferrule and change from one grip to another—even on occasion from one hand to another—to rest your muscles as you work.

Conventional brushes and rollers work fine on exterior surfaces that are smooth or only slightly textured. But there are some rough surfaces such as stucco, cinder block or wooden shingles that these ordinary applicators might not be able to handle. On such surfaces, even a deep-pile roller may miss spots that you then must fill in with a brush. But avoid the temptation to poke at a rough surface with the tip of the brush to work paint into the pores and crevices, a practice that quickly ruins the bristles.

There are also a number of specialized applicators for certain kinds of outdoor work. The three most useful ones, shown on the opposite page, are a pad applicator for shingles, a rectangular paintbrush that looks like a pad with bristles for masonry and a mitten applicator for railings and pipes.

Painting clapboards with a brush. The bottom edges of four or five clapboards are coated first, then the faces. Using a brush about as wide as a clapboard and dipping only the tip in paint, apply paint to 3-foot lengths of the clapboard edge (*top drawing*). Next, with a fully laden brush, apply heavy dabs of paint to the face of one clapboard (*center*). Distribute the paint across the wood with horizontal brush strokes (*bottom*). Finish off each clapboard with a single long horizontal stroke to eliminate brush marks, then proceed to the next clapboard. Use the same sequence when painting shingles, but apply the paint with vertical strokes to follow the grain of the wood.

The pad applicator. Designed for painting or staining shakes and shingles, a pad applicator consists of a soft "rug" of short nylon bristles that are attached to a layer of flexible foam rubber so the bristles conform to the uneven surfaces of the shingles as pressure is applied. This replaceable pad is secured to a plastic handle by fold-over metal tabs, and can be reversed to prolong the life of the bristles. To use a pad applicator, dip the bristles into a tray of paint or stain and apply the coating first to the edge of a shingle with the edge of the pad. Then press the entire pad firmly against the front of the shingle (*drawing, below*) and pull downward with a single stroke. The applicator can also be used to paint wide clapboards and other flat surfaces.

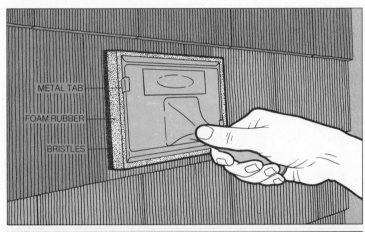

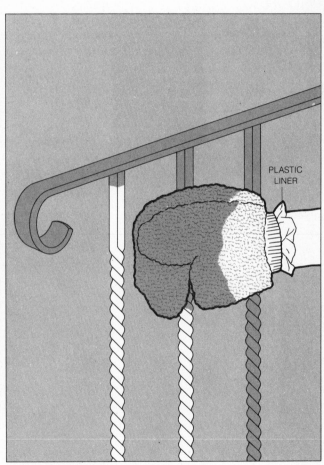

A rough-surface paintbrush. The stubby bristles of this brush are ideal for scrubbing paint, sealers or other coatings into the pores and crevices of cinder block, brick and stucco. Work the paint into the surface with a circular motion of the brush (*drawing*), then smooth it out with straight finishing strokes. This brush can also be used to paint shingles; the narrow row of bristles along the bottom is used to coat the edge of a shingle, and then the entire brush is used like a pad applicator to paint the face of the shingle.

A mitten applicator. Faster than any brush for coating pipes and railings, this applicator is a bulky mitten covered with lamb's wool on both sides so that it can be used on either hand. The palm of the mitten is dipped into a tray of paint, and then wiped onto the pipe or railing (*drawing*). A plastic liner, visible at the painter's wrist, keeps paint from seeping through the mitten onto his hand. The mitten can be cleaned and re-used just like any brush or roller.

Spray Painting: Fast but Tricky

Speed is the main attraction of spray painting. In less than a day an average-sized, two-story house with a garage can be sprayed with a coat of paint or stain that is almost the equivalent of two coats applied with brush or roller. To get this double coating, the sprayer will of course use nearly twice as much paint as if it were applied in the conventional way. If you do not need a double coat, thin the paint with the proper solvent.

There are two kinds of sprayers in general use. The traditional type uses compressed air to atomize paint and deposit it on a surface. A newer type, the airless sprayer shown on these pages, is generally considered most efficient for house exteriors. It forces liquid paint directly through the spray-gun nozzle under extremely high pressure. The high pressure can be dangerous, however; note the cautions in the box at right. With any sprayer, always wear a respirator mask, available at paint stores, to avoid inhaling paint or solvent mists.

You can rent spray gear by the day from many paint stores. But make sure there are no local ordinances that restrict outdoor spraying. Then, before you use the sprayer, prepare your house for painting as described on pages 61-69. Allot enough time—you may need a whole day —to mask everything that you want to protect from speckling. Park your car where a chance breeze cannot spatter paint over it. Once the house is masked, you can paint it on the first calm day.

Though airless equipment is surprisingly simple to use, make sure you receive written operating instructions—the manufacturer's instructions are best—when you rent the sprayer. Machines differ slightly in the way you set them up and clean them after the job.

The setup procedure is basically a matter of using the unit's pump to flush the sprayer with a solvent—water or mineral spirits—that is compatible with the paint, and then pumping paint through the hose to the gun. Cleanup is just the reverse. Pump remaining paint out of the hose, then flush the system with solvent.

For trouble-free spraying, make sure the spray tip has the correct size aperture for the coating you will be using. Thin liquids such as stains require a small-tip aperture; viscous fluids such as latex paint require a larger one. Ask for a tip that sprays a pattern about 8 inches high; this provides the best compromise between speed and accuracy of application.

To reduce the chance of the sprayer becoming clogged with foreign matter, strain the paint through two or three thicknesses of cheesecloth into a clean bucket. Then immerse the sprayer pickup tube in the paint and turn on the pump. Start with the pump set at its lowest pressure and test the sprayer against a large piece of cardboard or scrap plywood. Gradually increase the pressure, if necessary, until the gun produces an even pattern with no gaps.

To get the hang of actual spraying, practice on an inconspicuous part of the house where errors can be corrected with a paintbrush. After covering the area the size of a double-garage door, most people are proficient enough with an airless sprayer to do a professional-looking paint job on a house.

Safety Tips for Airless Sprayers

The pump of an airless sprayer pushes paint through its spray tip at pressures up to 3,000 pounds per square inch and at speeds up to 200 miles per hour —enough force to inject paint right through your skin and into your finger if it is held too close to a discharging nozzle. Such an injury is potentially dangerous. If any part of your body is hit at short range by an emerging jet of paint or solvent, seek immediate medical attention. A hospital emergency room is the best place to go; your family doctor may not know how to treat this special kind of wound effectively. Accidents need not occur, however, if you follow these few basic safety rules.

☐ Use only a spray gun that has a trigger guard, a safety lock and a safety shield around the spray tip. Keep the safety lock engaged when you are not actually spraying.

☐ Never point the gun at yourself or another person.

☐ Keep your fingers away from the spray tip. Never try to clear out the nozzle of a gun by pressing your finger against the spray tip while paint is being discharged.

☐ Do not disassemble airless equipment for any reason—to clean a spray tip or filter, for example—without first turning it off, unplugging it and then depressing the spray-gun trigger to release pressure in the hose.

☐ Keep children and pets away, and never leave the sprayer unattended.

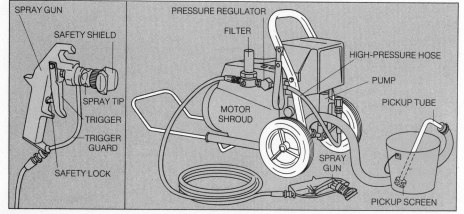

SPRAY GUN · SAFETY SHIELD · SPRAY TIP · TRIGGER · TRIGGER GUARD · SAFETY LOCK · PRESSURE REGULATOR · FILTER · HIGH-PRESSURE HOSE · PUMP · PICKUP TUBE · MOTOR SHROUD · SPRAY GUN · PICKUP SCREEN

The efficient airless sprayer. The heart of an airless sprayer is a hydraulic pump run by a powerful electric motor, which is concealed by a shroud on this model. The pump moves paint from a bucket through a pickup tube equipped with a coarse screen to trap foreign matter. The paint is then forced into a small-diameter, high-pressure hose, past a pressure regulator, which you adjust to produce an even spray pattern, and through a filter fine enough to capture particles that might clog the spray tip. Additional high-pressure hose, usually about 50 feet, carries the paint to the spray gun. The gun itself (*inset*) is equipped with a trigger guard and a safety lock to prevent accidental discharge and a safety shield to keep fingers from getting too close to the spray tip.

How to Spray

Spraying a uniform coat. The essential trick to spray painting is to hold the gun properly: perpendicular to the wall and 12 inches away. To maintain this constant angle and distance, crook your elbow slightly and bend your wrist (*drawing*), so that you can move the gun in a line exactly parallel to the wall. Never swing the spray tip in an arc as you would a garden hose—if you do, the spray pattern will expand and the coating will be uneven. For best results, do not spray a section wider than you can comfortably reach, no more than 36 inches for most painters.

Covering a wall. Spraying a series of smooth, overlapping strips is the most reliable method of achieving an even coat of paint over an entire wall. First spray a vertical strip down the edge of the wall, releasing the trigger at the end of the stroke. This strip keeps you from spraying past the edge and wasting paint when applying horizontal strips. For even coating, start the gun moving before depressing the trigger at the beginning of each stroke and keep it moving after releasing the trigger at the end. Each horizontal pass should overlap the previous strip and the vertical strip by about an inch to compensate for the thin coating at the ends of the spray pattern.

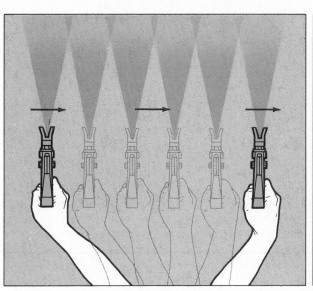

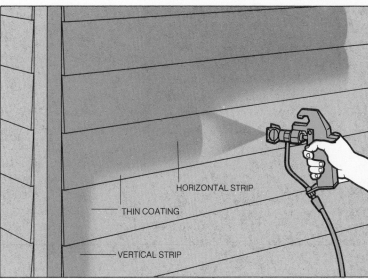

HORIZONTAL STRIP

THIN COATING

VERTICAL STRIP

Spraying the Wrong Way

The paint patterns illustrated at right are a tip-off that you are either holding or moving the spray gun incorrectly, producing coatings that are thicker in some places than in others. An hourglass pattern (*upper drawing*) results if you move the gun without bending your wrist to keep the sprayer the correct, 12-inch distance from the wall. As the gun arcs past the wall, it first moves closer to the wall and then farther away, leaving a wide thin coat at the ends of the strip and a narrow thick coat at the center.

Tilting the gun causes a different kind of unevenness (*lower drawing*). If the gun is pointed slightly downward, the resulting layer of paint will be denser at the top of the spray pattern than it is at the bottom; if the gun is pointed upward, the layer of paint will be applied too thickly along the bottom.

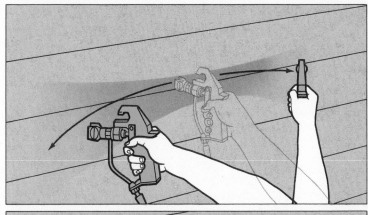

Wallpapering for Everyone

Wallpaper is not wallpaper anymore; it is wall covering—much of it is no longer simply printed paper but plastic, fabric or a combination. These newer materials are tougher and generally easier to handle than older types. They do not tear as readily, and many of them offer such labor-saving features as pretrimmed edges, factory-applied adhesive and reinforced backings (which simplify removal the next time redecorating is necessary). As a result, the once-arcane craft of paperhanging is today a routine job for the homeowner; according to one estimate, well over 60 per cent of the wall coverings sold are hung by the men and women who buy them.

These amateur paperhangers find in wallpaper an attractive alternative to paint. Hanging wallpaper is no more difficult than painting: the methods described in this chapter will help you achieve professional-looking results even if you never attempted the task before. Your main problem, indeed, may be choosing the right type and pattern of covering for your needs. Both factors affect not only appearance but ease of hanging and long-range durability.

Great toughness characterizes some special materials—cork and leather, for example—among the 13 types and 31 subtypes of wall coverings listed on pages 80-81. But of the commonly used wall coverings, the most durable are those made of a sheet of plastic bonded to cloth, the so-called fabric-backed vinyls. They are more scuff resistant and can be scrubbed more safely than a painted surface. Unbacked vinyl is a close second, followed by vinyl-coated paper, which, while less rugged than the others, is quite serviceable and somewhat easier to work with. Other types, from the textured grass cloths and common papers to the metalized foils and the fuzzy embossings of "flocked" papers, are considerably more fragile. These delicate coverings are less suitable for areas that are subject to heavy wear—kitchens, playrooms and children's bedrooms—and they also require extra care in hanging, since they are likely to tear or crease more readily than the vinyls.

Some of these types require special hanging procedures such as the use of lining paper *(page 122)*, an inexpensive, unpatterned material that is applied to the wall and then covered over with the paper that is meant to be seen. It absorbs moisture quickly, protecting coverings like grass cloth that tend to separate from their backings when wet; and it provides a smooth surface, even on a rough wall, for hanging highly reflective coverings such as foils.

The hanging of any type of wall covering is greatly simplified if the covering can be obtained prepasted—that is, with dry adhesive already on its back. You need only dip the paper into water to make the adhesive sticky and ready to put on the wall; you avoid the messy job of mixing and applying paste and setting up a table to work on. Most widely used wall coverings—vinyls, papers, foils and flocks—are available prepasted, but of course not all patterns in those types are supplied in this easy-to-use form.

The pattern itself has, beyond its obvious esthetic importance, a surprisingly large practical influence on the job. Some elaborate patterns may be impossible to use on ceilings *(page 108)*, and others introduce extra difficulties in matching at seams *(page 97)*. Even the manufacturing process employed in printing the pattern has an important effect. Most patterns fall into two categories, machine prints and hand prints. Less expensive patterns are machine-printed in large quantities on high-speed printing presses; the others are produced by hand by a process called silk screening.

In machine printing, all the wallpaper rolls cut from one continuous "run" are identical in color. The colors in earlier or later runs may vary slightly; therefore, manufacturers label each roll with a run or lot number. Be sure any machine-printed paper you buy has the same number, and ask the dealer to exchange unmatched rolls.

Hand prints cannot be matched for color as closely as machine prints because each roll is individually hand-screened and slight color variations occur from roll to roll. You must distribute strips of hand-printed paper on the walls in a way that makes the slight changes of shading least noticeable. Hand prints are fragile and are customarily sold with untrimmed edges, or selvages, to protect them in transit. Because of their fragility and higher cost, hand prints are best reserved for areas of comparatively little wear.

A color variation somewhat similar to that in hand-printed papers also affects grass cloths and similar materials. They are not printed, of course, acquiring their textured design from a surface of fibers supported on a paper backing. The fibers from which they are made do not respond evenly to dyes; color gradually lightens or darkens from one edge of a strip to the other, and varies along the length of the roll. Much of the charm of grass cloth arises from these shadings, but to avoid abrupt changes of color at the line where two adjacent strips meet, hang every other strip upside down, so that light edge will meet light edge and dark will meet dark.

Once you have chosen a material and a pattern, ask your dealer for a sample of the paper—a few square inches will do. Take it home and wet it by holding it briefly under a tap or by dunking it in water for a few seconds to simulate the conditions under which you will handle the paper after applying the paste. Test the sample to see how easily you can tear it; most papers will tear, but you should avoid those that tear too easily.

For your next test, rub the sample firmly with a damp sponge to see if the colors run; if they do—and they frequently will, especially in hand prints—you are dealing with an especially tricky paper. You will have to be extremely careful not to get adhesive on the patterned side of the paper because you will be unable to wash it off, and the standard practice of sponging off an entire strip after it has been hung must be omitted. After you have hung a paper that tends to run, you then can spray it with a transparent stain-resistant coating available at wallpaper stores; test the coating first on a large remnant to make sure that it will not smear the pattern.

If the sample passes these tests, buy enough paper for your needs, using the calculation described on page 87. You can make this estimate far more precisely than you can estimate paint needs—while the covering power of paint varies with the color, porosity and smoothness of a wall, a single roll of wallpaper will always cover approximately 30 square feet, whatever the condition of the wall. Do not stint on paper: the cost of an extra roll is insignificant compared to the unsightly result of completing a job with paper from a different print run. And if you end up with an unused roll, you may be able to return it for a refund; many dealers offer such a service. Buy the adhesive along with the paper, using the chart to find the adhesive most suitable for the type of covering you have chosen. Vinyl adhesive is recommended for heavy coverings because it makes an especially strong bond. If your project involves a lighter covering and calls for a wheat-paste adhesive, be sure that the material you buy contains an additive to prevent mildew, which causes unsightly stains. Because of the potential mildew problem, never hang a vinyl covering over a paper applied with wheat paste: vinyl is airtight, and it traps in the wall moisture that can produce mildew in the old coat of paste. The only safe procedure to follow in this situation is to remove all the old paper layers before applying the new one.

Before tackling a papering job, prepare all wall surfaces by the methods described on pages 84-86, and do whatever painting is necessary. Though not essential, a coat of wall size—a thin adhesive applied with a paint roller or paste brush—makes it easier to slide a wallpaper strip into place and facilitates removal at a later date. Finally, if you are not using a prepasted covering, mix the adhesive according to the manufacturer's directions.

After these preparations the rest of the job goes remarkably fast. You can easily paper an average bedroom in a day. Do not hurry the job, however; be thorough and methodical—this is the secret of the professional paperhanger.

When the job is done, you will have an accumulation of paper scraps, large and small. Discard creased pieces and small slivers, but keep the rest; as long as the paper remains on the walls, these remnants will be handy for patching a damaged spot or re-covering a soiled switch plate. You may find that the paper on the walls has faded while the remnants did not—but experts have worked out a solution to the problem. They recommend hanging large paper remnants over a clothesline in an attic; then the leftover paper fades at the same rate as the paper on the walls.

Choosing a Wall Covering

Type	How Sold	Where to Use
Common Papers Untreated Vinyl-coated Cloth-backed	Single, double and triple rolls, 18 to 27 inches wide; length and width always combine to provide 36 square feet per single roll, yielding at least 30 square feet after waste allowance	Areas of moderate wear, such as dining rooms and adult bedrooms
Vinyls Laminated to paper Laminated to woven fabric Impregnated cloth on paper backing Laminated to unwoven fabric	Same as common papers; heaviest grades also available in widths to 54 inches and lengths to 30 yards	All-purpose, heavy-wear areas, such as kitchens, bathrooms and children's rooms
Foils Simulated metallic Aluminum laminated to paper Aluminum laminated to cloth	Same as common papers	Decorative highlights; small alcoves or hallways
Flocks On paper On vinyl On foil	Same as common papers	Decorative highlights and formal areas; dining rooms, hallways
Prepasted Coverings Papers Vinyls Foils Flocks	Same as common papers	Same areas as similar nonprepasted coverings
Fabrics Untreated Laminated to paper Self-adhesive	Bolts usually 45 inches wide, but also in widths of 54 and 60 inches; sold by the yard	Decorative highlights; dining rooms, bedrooms, hallways
Felt Laminated to paper	Bolts 54 inches wide; sold by the yard	Decorative highlights; bedrooms; special effects
Textured Coverings Grass cloth Shiki silk Hemp Burlap	Double rolls, 36 inches wide and 24 feet long, except burlap, which also is available in widths to 54 inches	Living rooms, recreation rooms
Murals On paper On vinyl On foil	Strips 10 to 12 feet long, with matching paper for surrounding areas	Special effects
Cork Laminated to paper Laminated to burlap	Widths up to 36 inches, in 24-, 36- and 45-foot lengths	Small rooms; recreation rooms; decorative highlights
Laminated Wood Veneers Random patterns Matched veneers	Strips 10 to 24 inches wide and up to 12 feet long; end-matched strips for taller walls available on request from manufacturer	Substitute for wall paneling; dens, around fireplaces
Gypsum-coated Wall Fabric	Single rolls, 4 feet wide and 30 yards long	Covering for concrete blocks, masonry and damaged wall surfaces; basement recreation rooms
Leather	Single dressed hides; one large cowhide covers from 25 to 40 square feet	Special effects

Adhesives	Handling Hints	Special Comments
Wheat paste or stainless cellulose paste	Follow basic procedures (*pages 92-103*); treat carefully to avoid rips	Susceptible to grease stains and abrasions; pattern inks may run if washed; strippable if cloth-backed
Mildew-resistant type; vinyl compound suggested	Does not stick to itself, double-cut all overlaps (*page 99*)	Most durable type currently available; may be scrubbed; almost always strippable
Mildew-resistant type; vinyl compound suggested	Hang over lining paper (*page 122*) to minimize wall defects; avoid wrinkles, which cannot be smoothed	Fragile and hard to handle; may cause glare in sunny areas; available in striking supergraphics
Same as for corresponding unflocked paper, vinyl or foil, but slightly thicker	Vacuum loose flock particles before applying adhesive; hang over lining paper to ensure smooth surface	Vinyl flocks washable; all may be damaged by excessive rubbing
Water-activated, applied at factory	Use water box (*page 93*); follow manufacturer's instructions for soaking	Ideal for the inexperienced
Powdered vinyl adhesive or double-faced vinyl tape if fabric is untreated; wheat paste or stainless cellulose paste if laminated	Paint all woodwork before hanging; hang over lining paper; stretch fabric until taut, but not out of shape	Easy to clean with dry-cleaning fluids or powders
Wheat paste	Hang over lining paper; hang strips with nap in the same direction; avoid paste smears, which cause felt to pucker and fade when cleaned	May be vacuumed, but stains are hard to remove; some colors fade
Wheat paste or stainless cellulose paste	Reverse every other strip top for bottom to prevent abrupt changes of shading; avoid excess moisture, which causes fibers to separate from backing; hang over lining paper for faster drying	All available in either natural or synthetic fibers; Shiki silk, a fine grass-cloth type, also sold in overprinted designs
Same as for corresponding paper, vinyl or foil	Hang over lining paper (*page 122*) to ensure smooth surface	Muslin or unbleached cotton may be substituted for lining paper to create strippable mural
Wheat paste if laminated to paper; prepared vinyl adhesive if laminated to burlap	Hang over lining paper; requires no matching	Keep well vacuumed; all cork surfaces are washable; cork absorbs and deadens sounds within a room
Specified by manufacturer	Set room temperature to 70° F. or higher for fast drying; use manufacturer's recommended sequence when hanging matched veneers	Fire-resistant; allowed by strictest city codes where solid wood paneling is banned
Supplied by manufacturer	Set room temperature to 70° F. or higher for fast drying; reverse every other strip, top for bottom	Dries to plaster-like surface; available only in pastel shades, but may be painted in other colors
Mildew-resistant type; vinyl compound suggested	Cut into simple shapes such as squares, rectangles and triangles and arrange into an attractive pattern to fit the area; polish with paste floor wax	Expensive, handsome and durable; stains are difficult, but can be removed by brushing on rubber cement and peeling it off

Tool Kit for Paperhanging

Not every tool in the collection at right is used in every job—the water box, for example, is needed only for prepasted papers—and some, like the trimming knife and the cutting wheel, are interchangeable. Buy only what is necessary for the wall covering you choose.

☐ To remove an old covering from a wall, a paper stripper breaks the surface of a covering to prepare it for wetting. The flexible wall scraper finishes the job of removing the covering from the wall. You need a rigid putty knife if the walls must be patched before the new covering is applied.

☐ The tools for hanging paper make up most of the rest of the kit. Use a metal straightedge at least a yard long to take measurements and to guide long, straight cuts like those that trim edges. The cutting is done with scissors or a utility knife; for trimming, use a trimming guide and a cutting wheel or trimming knife (keep single-edge razor blades on hand for the knife, since the blades dull rapidly).

☐ You have to draw a precisely vertical line on the wall before hanging the first strip of paper and several times thereafter; the job is simplified by the plumb bob shown here, which has a pull-out string that automatically coats itself with chalk from a reservoir in the case.

☐ A metal or plastic paste bucket and a paste brush are used to mix and apply adhesive. Keep a second bucket for clear water, and a clean sponge to wash off excess adhesive after you have hung each strip. To fix the paper firmly on the wall, use a smoothing brush with ¾-inch bristles for a stiff vinyl or 2-inch bristles for a more pliable covering. A seam roller gives a final smoothing to edges.

☐ Fewer tools are needed for a prepasted paper: you can eliminate the paste brush and paste bucket, and a sponge is generally recommended for smoothing instead of the brush and seam roller. You will, however, have to buy a water box.

☐ Both the trimming knife and the seam roller may be needed for minor repairs on previously hung paper if its edges become loose. If you must eliminate an air bubble, use a thin artist's brush to apply adhesive or water under the paper.

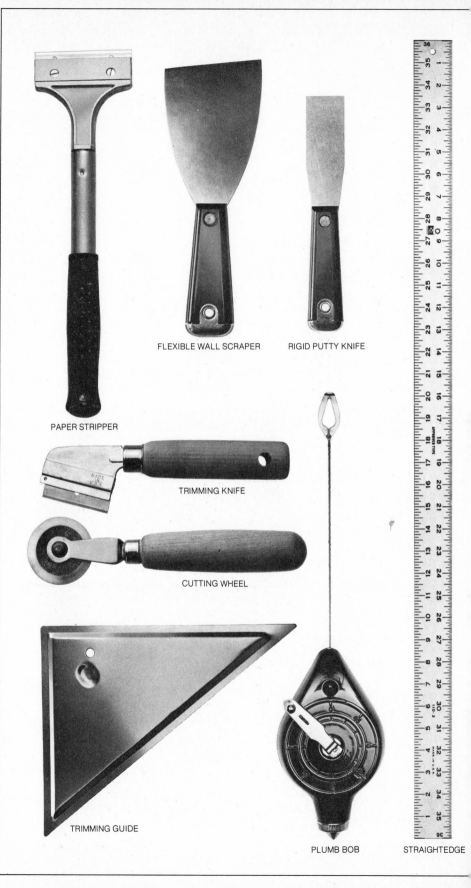

FLEXIBLE WALL SCRAPER   RIGID PUTTY KNIFE

PAPER STRIPPER

TRIMMING KNIFE

CUTTING WHEEL

TRIMMING GUIDE

PLUMB BOB   STRAIGHTEDGE

SPONGE

SMOOTHING BRUSH FOR VINYLS

SMOOTHING BRUSH FOR NONVINYLS

PASTE BRUSH

WATERCOLOR BRUSH

SEAM ROLLER

SCISSORS

UTILITY KNIFE

PASTE BUCKET

WATER BOX

The Three Ways to Remove Old Paper from the Walls

The first step in wallpapering a room is generally painting: if you plan to refinish the trim or paint the ceiling, complete this operation before starting anything else to avoid smudges on the walls. While it is simple to wipe wallpaper paste from woodwork, cleaning paint from new wallpaper is next to impossible. Next, clear the room, leaving space for a pasting table if you plan to apply wallpaper adhesive yourself.

Remove or loosen all objects attached to the walls exactly as if you were preparing to paint (page 20). You need not cover furniture as carefully as you would for a paint job, but be sure to spread several layers of newspaper over your work area to protect the floor from paste, water and sticky strips of old paper, if you are removing it before applying a new covering. To avoid having to drive new fastener holes for pictures or mirrors, insert a toothpick or a small nail in each hole as you remove the hook or screw. When you paper, these projections will puncture the covering and serve as markers when you rehang your decorations.

At this point, you have taken everything off the walls but old paint or paper. Paint presents no problem—you paper over it, though strippable paper should not be applied over latex paint—apply an oil- or alkyd-base coat for this type of covering. Most flat coats (except for calcimine or casein, which must be washed off) need no special preparation. Glossy finishes should be sponge-mopped or washed with a detergent (commercial floor-cleaning products are excellent) or a commercial deglosser to provide tooth —the roughness of surface needed for good adhesion. Because deglossers are usually strong solvents with toxic fumes, treat them as you would paint; let fresh air circulate in the room.

However, papering over paper, though possible, is risky: the water in wallpaper paste can loosen old layers so they pull away from the wall. Never attempt to paper over more than three layers of paper, no matter how well they seem to be attached. The weight of the additional layer, plus wet wallpaper paste, can pull away the whole sheaf of papers.

If you decide to paper over paper—because the wall beneath is too fragile to withstand paper stripping, or because the time you save by leaving the old paper on the wall is more important that the long-term durability of the finished job —make sure that the old covering is firmly attached to the wall and as smooth as possible. Tear away loosened strips of paper, feathering edges as for a repair job (page 118). Sand down lapped seams with coarse sandpaper; glue down curling corners with wallpaper paste. If you must paper over a shiny material such as vinyl or foil, either hand-sand or roughen the surface with a commercial liquid preparation that provides tooth.

In most cases, it is wiser to remove old paper; new coverings will always adhere better to a stripped wall. It is fairly easy to strip existing wall covering away if the material is vinyl or vinyl-coated cloth or paper, the most common wall coverings. These materials are easily identified by their rather smooth plastic texture. But if a test pull at a top corner gets no results, you are probably dealing with a nonstrippable material and will have to soak, steam or dry-strip the covering from the wall. The tools you will need are a paper stripper, a 3- to 4-inch-wide scraper or flexible putty knife, sponges, water, and possibly an electric wallpaper steamer.

The stripping method depends largely on the structural material of the wall beneath the covering. You can identify this material by drilling a small hole, not more than ¼ inch wide and 1 inch deep. If your drill bit produces white dust and meets steady, moderate resistance, the wall is made of plaster. But to make sure the steady resistance is not caused by drilling into a stud, drill a second hole 6 or 8 inches away on a diagonal—it should give the same results. Brown dust and moderate resistance, followed by a sudden "pop" as the drill drives through to the hollow space within the wall, indicates wood or such wood products as particle board or hardboard paneling. White dust, little resistance and a quick pop of the drill are the signs of gypsum board.

If the wall is made of plaster or wood, old wall covering can be soaked off (top, far right) or, if it resists soaking, steamed off (page 86). These methods will not work on gypsum board, because the moisture produced by soaking or steaming softens the kraft-paper covering of the board, and subsequent scraping to remove paper destroys the board's plaster core. Instead, use the stripping tool shown in Step 1 of the soaking process (top, right) to dry-strip the paper.

Once you have stripped the paper, prepare the walls so that the new paper will both adhere well and come off easily the next time you redecorate. First, repair damaged surfaces as described on pages 20-21. Then paint gypsum board, hardboard and particle board with a flat alkyd primer. Latex primer is least costly for priming wallboard, but foil, vinyl, mylar and most dry-strippable coatings will not adhere to it. Cover raw wood with lining paper (page 122) to prevent the grain of the wood, which the water in wallpaper paste can raise, from showing through the new covering as a series of ripples and bumps.

Finally, seal unprimed or papered walls to prevent paste from being absorbed into them and to provide a surface that the paper will glide onto easily. The least costly sealer is the glue called wallpaper size, available in liquid or powder form. A quart of either, mixed with water according to package directions, covers about 300 square feet. But glue-and-resin and straight resin sealers, designed especially as a base for wall coverings, are more versatile, though a quart will cover only about 150 square feet. They provide tooth without sanding on such slick surfaces as ceramic tile and glass, form a water barrier on gypsum board so that the paper you apply can later be soaked or steamed off without damage to the wall, and they seal plaster patches against the adhesion-destroying alkalis that rise to the surface of fresh masonry. (If you use glue size, locate and remove alkaline areas—"hot spots"—by the method shown on page 87.)

Apply size or resin sealer with a brush or roller just as you would paint, making sure that no patches of wall are left bare. When a wall is particularly absorbent or rough, glue size can be mixed with slightly less than the manufacturer's recommended amount of water for a thicker covering. Or apply two thin coats of size. Since appearance does not matter, the job will be a quick one.

Slitting and Soaking

1 Preparing the paper. Most papers can be wet through easily, but slick, nonporous coverings may need to be punctured before they can be soaked. Roughen them with coarse sandpaper or a wire brush, or pierce them with a stripper to let in water. Hold the blade of this tool perpendicular to the wall and, applying gentle pressure *(drawing)*, slit the paper horizontally at intervals of 8 to 10 inches. The same tool can be used to dry-strip paper from gypsum board. First slit the wall covering, then slide the blade into the slit at an angle and loosen a section of paper at a time. Tear the loosened sections off with your fingers.

2 Wetting the paper. Using a large sponge *(drawing)*, with a firm, circular motion, wet a strip of paper with warm water and detergent to soften the old paste. If the paste is especially water resistant, use a liquid paper remover—a solution of ethyl alcohol and other chemicals or a liquid containing enzymes that break down the organic materials in wallpaper paste. Use rubber gloves with liquid paper remover. Let the strip soak for five to 10 minutes. Then resoak it and give the adjoining strip a first soak. While waiting for water to penetrate the second strip, proceed to Steps 3 and 4 *(below)* on the first strip.

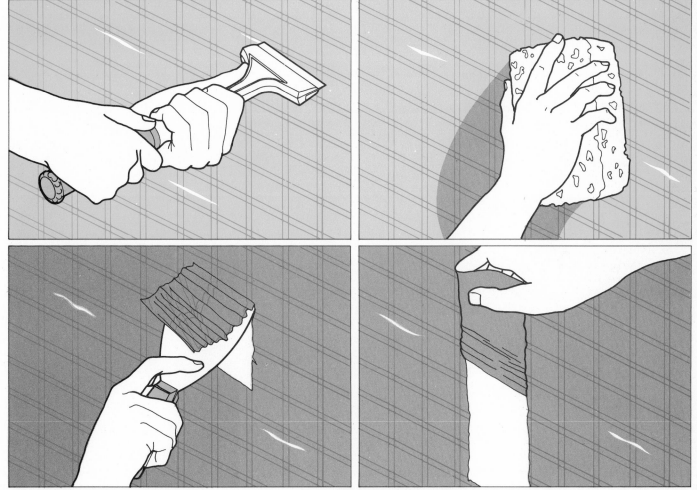

3 Scraping off the paper. Holding a flexible-blade, 3½-inch-wide wall scraper at about a 30° angle away from the wall *(drawing)*, firmly push the wet paper up from the bottom of the strip or from one of the horizontal slits made by a stripper. The paper should wrinkle in exactly the way that a wet jelly-jar label does when you push against it with a fingernail. If it does not, resoak and try again. If the paste is still resistant you will have to use a steamer *(page 86)*.

4 Stripping paper away. Grasp the loosened paper with your fingers and tear upward with a steady, firm motion *(drawing)*. Do not pull the paper outward: it may rip off in your hand before a sizable section has been removed. Paper that is uncoated will tear less evenly than vinyl-coated wall coverings, but both types of paper should peel away easily in long strips. After stripping off all the paper in the room, wash the walls down with warm water to remove any of the remaining scraps of wallpaper and paste.

Using an Electric Wallpaper Steamer

1 **Starting the steamer.** Some papers do not respond to the method shown on page 85. An electric steamer will probably do the job, for vapor will penetrate where water cannot. A steamer, for rent at most wallpaper dealers, typically consists of a perforated plate connected by a hose to a water tank, heated by an electric coil in its base. To fill the tank, make sure the cord is unplugged and remove the stopper valve at the top. Set a funnel in the opening and pour in boiling water until the water-level gauge indicates full. Plug in the steamer; a pilot light shows when the unit is on. The steamer is ready to use when vapor comes from the steamer plate.

2 **Using the steamer plate.** When steam pours steadily from the perforations in the steamer plate, hold it firmly against the wall. Do not move the plate in any direction. In two or three minutes you will see the paper around the plate dampen and darken, and water droplets may start to run down the wall. Move the plate onto an adjacent area in the same strip of paper and repeat the steaming process. When you have steamed half a strip, proceed to Steps 3 and 4 of the removal procedure shown on page 85.

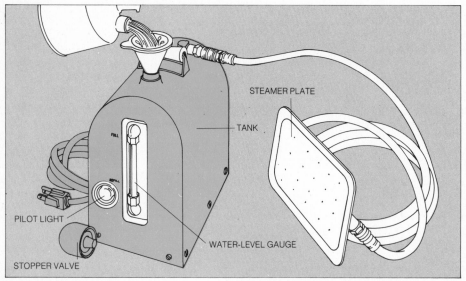

STEAMER PLATE

TANK

PILOT LIGHT

WATER-LEVEL GAUGE

STOPPER VALVE

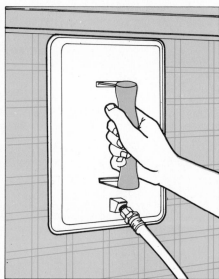

Paper That Peels Off

Removing strippable wall coverings. Many vinyl and vinyl-coated coverings and some mylars and fabrics can be stripped from walls dry. Use a fingernail or a utility knife to pull away a corner of the covering at the top of a section, and carefully peel the covering downward, pulling it flat against itself. If you pull the covering outward and away from the wall, its paper backing may rip unevenly, leaving a rough surface. Do not remove any fuzzy residue that is left by the backing; it will help the next coat of paste stick better.

Hot Spots and Their Treatment

Neutralizing alkalis. Alkali patches—called hot spots by paperhangers—are present in all fresh plaster and many old plaster walls. Because they keep wallpaper paste from sticking, they must be found and treated with alkali-canceling acid. A plaster repair patch is easy to see; hot spots on larger areas become visible when glue size is applied—they turn pink, red or purple (blue tint in drawing at right). Neutralize these spots with a solution of one part 28 per cent acetic acid and two parts water. Wearing rubber gloves, swab this mixture over the spot with a soft cloth. The color will fade gradually; when it disappears completely, the alkali is gone; finish by resizing the area.

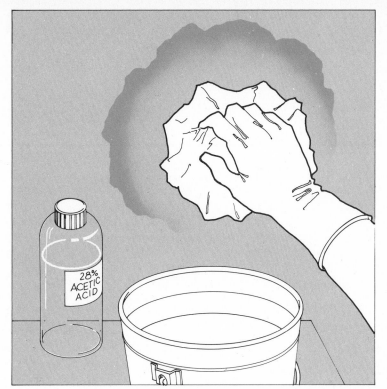

28%
ACETIC
ACID

How Much Paper? How Much Time?

Wallpaper is manufactured in "runs"—long strips are printed from a single dye batch. Then the dye is replaced and another long strip—up to several thousand feet—is printed. This method may result in slight color variations from run to run. And because of these color variations, it is best not to hazard a guess at the amount of paper you will need. Rather than run short in mid-job and risk a bad match, buy all the paper you need at one time.

To calculate the amount of paper necessary to cover your room, find the room perimeter as you would for a paint job *(page 13)*. Multiply that figure by room height measured from the baseboard to the ceiling—or to a cornice, if you do not mean to paper above it—then subtract the exact area of doors, windows and other places you will not paper. The final figure will be a close estimate of the wall area of the room. If you plan to paper the ceiling as well, find the area of the floor; if it does not duplicate the ceiling (because of dormers or bay windows, for example), you may have to allow for cutbacks or ex-

tensions. Use a ladder to measure these areas and add them to the floor figure.

Wall coverings are measured in units called single rolls. Though the width of papers may range from 15 to 54 inches, a single roll contains approximately 36 square feet of covering. Despite this standard unit of measurement, most papers are sold in double-length rolls called bolts and some are sold in three- or four-roll bolts.

You must expect to waste about 6 square feet per single roll on odd-shaped areas, on points where the wall ends before your pattern does, and in trimming excess paper from the top and bottom of a strip. Therefore, divide your total wall or ceiling area by 30 square feet to find the number of single-roll units you will need.

You should request that your paper be delivered in two-, three- or four-roll bolts cut in continuous, long strips. Working from a bolt of this length, you can cut as many as five or six floor-to-ceiling strips with ease and minimal waste. However, unless the actual number of rolls you need turns out to be an

exact multiple of two or three, try to avoid paper that is sold only in bolts. If you should need to cover a small area calling for just one extra roll and you have only multiple-roll bolts, you could wind up wasting from one to three full rolls. But don't underbuy if you have no choice; it might be difficult or impossible to match your paper later.

If you are hanging on bare or painted walls in good condition, allow a full day to size and paper a 12-by-15-foot room. If the walls need substantial repairs, or if you must remove an existing coat of paper, double that estimate, especially if you are papering for the first time. But you need not feel that a papering job must be an extended and exhausting effort. Unlike painting, papering can be done piecemeal. If you are using prepasted paper there are no problems with paste preparation and cleanup; in any case, prepared paste can be saved till later *(page 92)*. If you must work in short spells, you can easily hang a strip or two and then leave the work—even for days if necessary—without harming the final effect.

Deciding Where to Start and Where to End

Because wallpaper must be hung in consecutive strips, with the pattern of each one matching a previously completed section, placement of the first strip governs the appearance of the finished job. Designs with narrow stripes and small random patterns do not cause matching problems; they can be started conveniently alongside any door or window. But before you begin to hang a complex pattern, you must choose your starting point carefully.

Complex patterns usually look best when the overall arrangement is symmetrical and the strips are placed so that the pattern draws the attention of a viewer to one part of a room: one wall, for example, or the space above a fireplace or the area surrounding one or more windows. When planning such an arrangement, it is wise to avoid having to hang strips narrower than 6 inches, because they may be difficult to align and affix. The instructions that follow explain how this problem can be minimized.

Keep in mind that a pattern may not necessarily be centered on the roll. In such cases, inspect the paper and note where the center of the pattern lies. But be aware that "drop-match patterns" (page 97) may not repeat horizontally until after two consecutive strips of the paper have been hung.

Make a light pencil mark on the wall where you want to center the overall pattern. Then, make a second mark to the left of the first mark at a distance equal to that between the center of the pattern on the roll and the left edge of the roll. You will want to hang the first strip with its left edge against this second mark; this will center the pattern precisely where you want it.

Unless the perimeter of the room is an exact multiple of the width of the pattern—an unlikely occurrence—there will probably be an unavoidable mismatch along one edge of the last strip that is to be hung. This will not happen in a room that has one surface interrupted by a floor-to-ceiling storage unit or a built-in corner cabinet. But in all rooms where four continuous walls are to be papered, you should plan ahead to locate the one inevitable mismatch so that you can contrive to have it happen in an inconspicuous place (page 90).

Locating the First Strip

To center on a wall. With a pencil, mark the center of the wall. Using a roll of wallpaper as a yardstick, measure the distance to the nearest corner. Start by placing one edge of the roll against the mark, then move the roll toward the corner, one width at a time, until less than one roll width remains. If this remaining distance is 6 inches or less (right, above), plan to center the first strip of paper over the mark (right, below). If the remaining distance exceeds 6 inches, hang the first strip of paper where you started measuring—with the left edge of the strip against the pencil mark. To center the pattern above a fireplace, make the pencil mark above the center of the mantelpiece and proceed as for a wall.

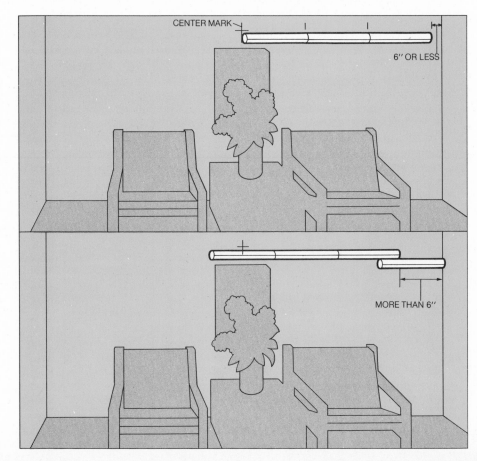

To center between two windows. The width of the wall between the windows will determine the placement of the first strip of wallpaper. With a pencil, mark a spot halfway between the windows and center a roll on that mark. If you find that centering the roll of paper on the mark would result in having narrow strips at each window edge (*left, below*), you may prefer to hang the first strip alongside the center mark (*right*).

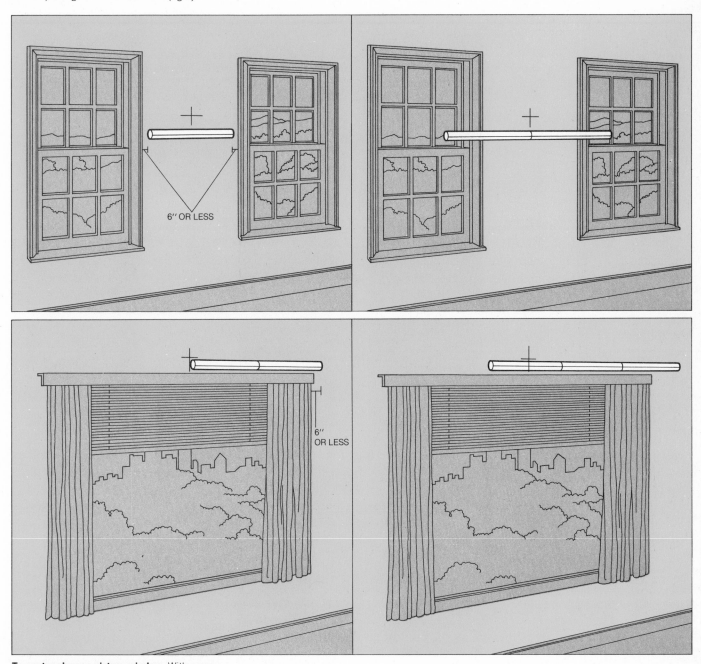

6" OR LESS

6" OR LESS

To center above a picture window. With a pencil, mark the center of the wall section above the window and measure as for walls (*opposite*), moving the roll toward the window's right upper corner. If the last full roll extends 6 inches or less beyond the corner of the window (*left, above*), plan to center the strip on the mark (*right*).

Locating the Last Strip

To end in a partly hidden area. You may find an unobtrusive corner where ending the wallpaper in mid-pattern will not be noticeable. In the room below, for example, the shallow corner where the fireplace meets the wall gets no direct light from the nearest window and is inconspicuous from most directions. Thus it is a suitable place to end. Another option might be one of the corners of the room itself—if it is hidden by furniture.

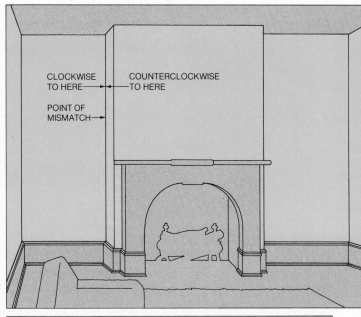

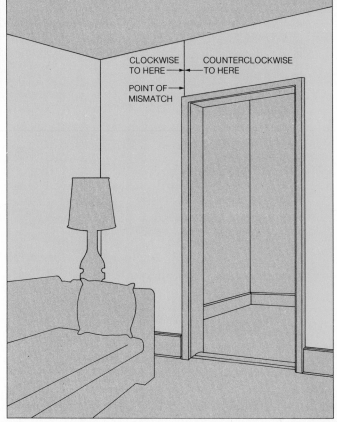

To end at a floor-to-ceiling interruption. If the wall you plan to paper is interrupted by a section of paneling, a fireplace or a built-in bookcase that goes from floor to ceiling, as in the illustration above, make this area the target of your final strip. Once you have chosen the location of your first strip *(pages 88-89)*, work from there both clockwise and counterclockwise, ending at the left and right sides of the interrupted area. In this way, there will be no mismatched strip anywhere.

To end above a door. The narrow strip of wall above a door is often one of the least conspicuous features of a room. You should make the last two strips meet above the left or right side of the door, whichever is closer to the room's nearest corner *(right)*. If, however, the door is centered on the wall, take into account the location of windows and lamps, and choose the side of the door that receives the least light.

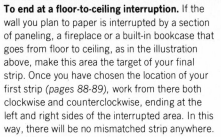

A Plumb Line to Get the Pattern Straight

No house has truly vertical walls. If you hang successive strips of wallpaper while merely following the planes of the walls, the room may look tipsy by the time you finish the job.

You can avoid slanted strips by drawing a true vertical line against which to align the first strip. Also, recheck the alignment after hanging every few strips, particularly after turning a corner; doing so will enable you to correct the alignment before the adhesive dries. Two alternative methods of marking a vertical line on a wall are illustrated at right, one using a plumb bob and the other using a metal straightedge. If you own a carpenter's level, you can use it instead of the straightedge; read both the upper and lower vials to make sure that the level is truly vertical. Press the level firmly against the wall and draw a pencil line along the side of the level.

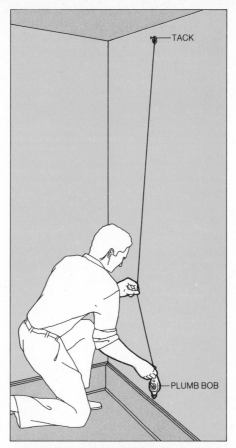

PLUMB BOB

TACK

Plumb bob and chalk. Rub colored chalk on a plumb-bob string (*pages 82-83*) and, with a thumbtack or small nail, attach the string to a point high on the wall. Wait until the bob stops swinging; the string will then be vertical. Without altering the bob's position, pull it slightly downward until the string is taut, press it firmly against the wall and snap the string with the other hand (*drawing*). This action will deposit a lightly colored vertical chalk line on the wall.

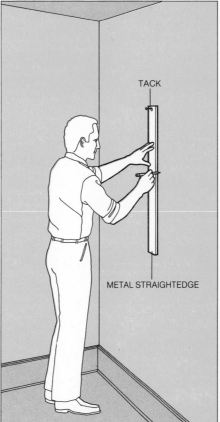

TACK

METAL STRAIGHTEDGE

Metal straightedge. If your metal straightedge (*pages 82-83*) has a hole at one end, tack it loosely to the wall through that hole. Let the straightedge dangle freely until it comes to rest; hold it firmly against the wall in that position and draw a light pencil line along its edge. The pencil line will be a true vertical (*drawing*).

A Mess-free Pasting Method

Unless you use prepasted paper and a water box *(opposite)*, the proper choice of an adhesive and its correct application have much to do with the success of a wallpapering project. The wall covering you buy is frequently accompanied by the manufacturer's instructions for the adhesive to be used; if not, follow the recommendations of your dealer.

Adhesives, whether organic or synthetic, are available in both liquid and dry form. The liquids are poured directly into a bucket if you plan to use a paste brush, or into a roller tray if you use a paint roller. Dry substances must first be mixed with water; directions on the package indicate the amount of water required. About 30 minutes before use, pour the powder slowly into the water to minimize lumps. Mix thoroughly and make sure that all lumps are completely dis-

solved. Store the leftover adhesive in an airtight container for future use.

As you apply the paste, spread it evenly and cover the entire surface of the strip. Avoid getting paste on the pattern side—or on the table where the next strip of wallpaper would come in contact with it. One simple way of preventing this is to spread several layers of paper on the table, discarding the top layer after applying the paste to each strip. Avoid using newspapers, however, since printer's ink may rub off onto the pattern. Substituting layers of kraft paper solves that problem, though it is relatively expensive, since each layer is used only once. The method demonstrated step by step on these pages eliminates entirely the need for layers of paper, by keeping the brush well away from the table surface during the entire operation.

1 **Pasting the lower left area.** After you have measured and cut the wallpaper into strips *(page 94)*, lay one strip with its pattern side down on the table. Allow the top end of the strip to hang over the table's edge. Slide the strip into position *(drawing)*; the strip's left and lower edges now extend beyond the table by a quarter of an inch or so. Paste the lower left quarter.

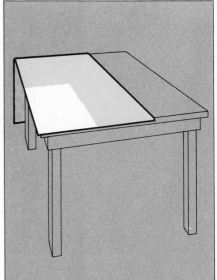

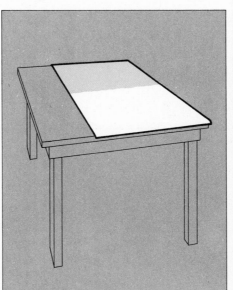

2 **Pasting the lower right area.** Shift the strip to the opposite long edge of the table with the strip's right and lower edges slightly over the edges. Paste the lower right quarter.

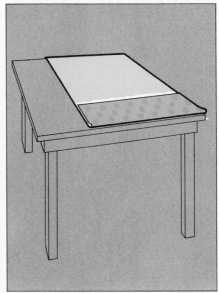

3 **Making the lower fold.** Pull the strip slightly toward you and gently fold the pasted section over on itself, pattern side out. Do not crease the fold. Make this fold somewhat shorter than the fold you will make at the top *(Step 6)* so that you will be able to identify the top when you are ready to hang the strip.

4 **Pasting the upper right area.** Slide the strip toward you until the upper edge of the paper barely overlaps the table. Make sure that the right edge of the paper still extends beyond the right edge of the table. The section of the strip that was previously pasted should now hang freely over the edge of the table. Paste the upper right quarter of the strip.

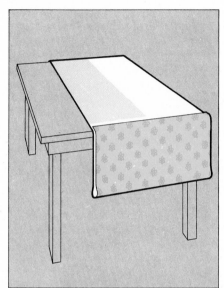

Using a Water Box

When using a prepasted paper, by all means get a special plastic container called a water box from your local wallpaper dealer. An inexpensive item, it will simplify your job.

Fill about two thirds of the box with water and place the box atop layers of newspaper, directly below each section of wall as you are working on it. After cutting a strip to the proper length, roll it loosely from bottom to top, with the pattern inside, then lay it in the box to soak for the length of time recommended by the manufacturer—usually 10 seconds to one minute. If the paper floats to the surface, slip an object without sharp edges —such as a wooden dowel—inside the rolled strip to weight it down.

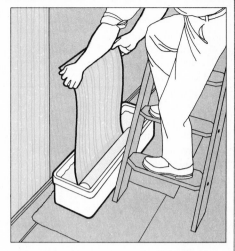

Pulling out the strip. Place your stepladder sideways in front of the water box. With the pattern facing you, draw the paper up as you climb the ladder. Hang the paper immediately.

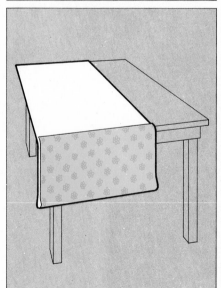

5 **Pasting the upper left area.** Shift the strip to the opposite long edge of the table until the strip's left and upper edges hang slightly over the edges. Paste the upper left quarter.

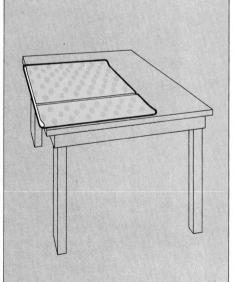

6 **Making the top fold.** After drawing the strip partly off the table, fold the upper section over on itself, pattern side out, so the top edge barely meets the bottom edge. Do not crease the fold. Set the pasted strip on a clean surface to cure for about 10 minutes; apply paste to additional strips while the first is curing. The strip will then be ready to hang (*pages 94-95*).

Putting Up the First Strip

After you have decided on placement of the first strip *(pages 88-89),* cut a length of wallpaper at least 4 inches longer than the height of the wall; the extra inches provide a trim allowance at the ceiling and baseboard. Apply paste and let it cure as explained on pages 92-93.

If the wallpaper has selvages—blank strips along both edges—remove them *(Step 1, below).* Usually, however, selvages have been trimmed off at the factory or the store. Some wallpaper is sold with perforations separating the selvages from the pattern; in such cases, you can knock the selvage off by rapping each end of the roll sharply against the edge of a table.

In hanging the first strip your primary concern should be to keep the strip rigorously vertical *(below, right).* Do not align the paper with the edge of a doorframe or the corner line of room walls;

such structural elements are almost certain to deviate from the true vertical in even the best-built house. Instead, mark a plumb line, as shown on page 91.

As you smooth the paper, avoid air bubbles—especially large ones; the brush strokes diagramed in Step 6 will eliminate all large bubbles and most small ones. The remaining small bubbles usually vanish as the paper dries (for any that persist, see page 120 for instructions on how to correct the problem).

As soon as the strip has been hung and trimmed—before the paste dries—use a clean sponge wrung in clear water to remove paste remaining on the ceiling, the baseboard and the face of the strip itself. Rinse the sponge often.

Although a smoothing brush is used to apply wallpaper in the steps that are illustrated here, a sponge or a paint roller works equally well.

The First Strip

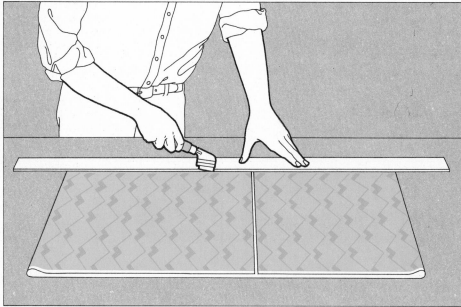

1 Trimming the selvages. If your paper has selvages, align the side edges of the pasted and folded strip, making sure that the visible portions of the selvages lie precisely over the hidden selvages on the underside of the folds. Exactly cover the visible selvage on one side with a straightedge. Using the straightedge as a guide, cut off the selvage with a firm, continuous stroke of your trimming knife or any sharp utility knife. Repeat the procedure on the other side of the strip.

2 Starting the alignment. Unfold the top section of the strip. Starting at the ceiling line, and allowing roughly 2 inches for final trimming along the ceiling, align one of the side edges of the paper with the plumb line *(drawing).* As you align the paper, pat the top section into place with your hand, just lightly enough to make it hold on the wall. Because wallpaper may stretch after it is dampened with paste or soaked in a water box, be careful not to pull the edges of the strip.

3 Brushing at the ceiling line. Use short, upward strokes of your smoothing brush to press the topmost few inches of paper against the wall, up to —but not beyond—the ceiling line. Work in this fashion across the entire width of the strip, pressing the paper firmly with the smoothing brush into the angle formed between ceiling and wall.

4 Brushing on the top section. With brisk, light strokes, press the entire top section of the strip against the wall, stopping an inch or so from the upper edge of the lower fold. Do not worry at this stage about occasional air bubbles. However, to avoid wrinkles, gently pull the lower part of the strip away from the wall up to the point where a wrinkle has formed and brush the paper smooth.

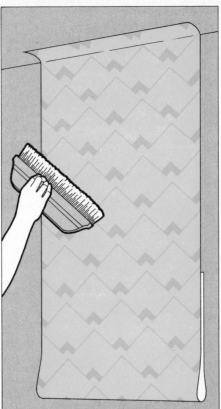

6 Smoothing the strip. Remove all air bubbles and ensure a firm bond between the paper and the wall with firm brush strokes—using both hands on the brush if necessary. Smooth the paper from the middle of the strip toward its edges, following the general direction of the arrows in the diagram and working from the top to the bottom. This technique will remove the air trapped in bubbles by forcing it out the sides of the strip. If any wrinkles appear while you are brushing the paper down or toward the edges, remove them as you did in Step 4. Finally, go over the entire surface of the strip with firm, vertical strokes.

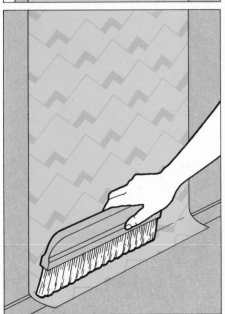

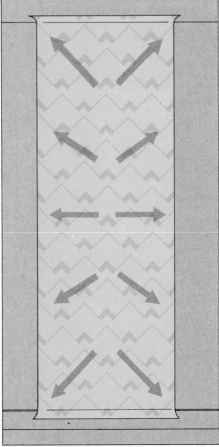

5 Applying the lower section. Unfold the lower section of the strip and continue aligning it against the plumb line down to the baseboard. Apply this part of the strip to the wall as in Step 4, using light brush strokes and avoiding wrinkles.

Trimming the Strip

1 Creasing. Press the wallpaper against the upper edge of the baseboard with the blunt side of a pair of scissors (*drawing*). The pressure of the scissors creases the paper along the line where the paper is to be trimmed.

2 Cutting. Gently lift the strip away from the wall and use scissors to cut off the excess along the crease you have made in Step 1. Brush the paper down again with your smoothing brush.
Repeat Steps 1 and 2 along the ceiling line.

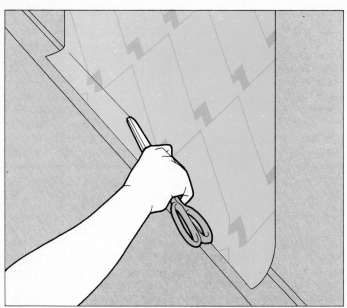

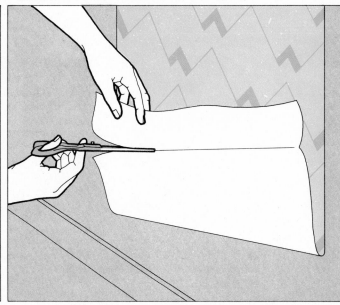

Other Ways to Trim

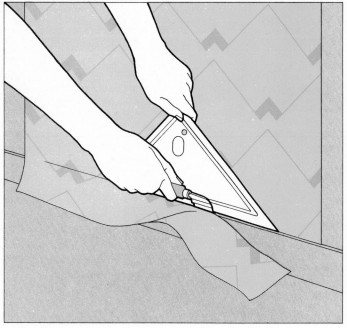

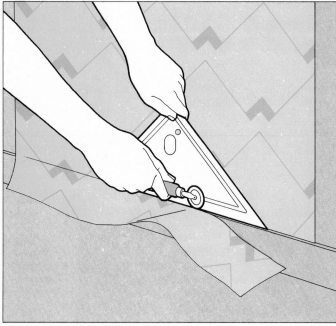

A trimming knife. Instead of using scissors, you may prefer to use a trimming knife, particularly in places where pulling the strip away from the wall would be awkward, such as around windows. Use a guiding edge such as a metal triangle (sold in paint stores) to ensure a straight cutting stroke and change the razor blade frequently.

A cutting wheel. For trimming fragile papers, which even a sharp knife might tear, use a cutting wheel. Handle the wheel as you would the trimming knife, rolling it along a guiding edge.

Matching the Basic Patterns: Straight and Drop

Except for those decorated solely with textures or stripes, wall-covering strips must be matched at their edges, and this requirement has to be taken into account in cutting every strip after the first. Patterns fall generally into two categories called "straight match" *(below, top)* and "drop match" *(bottom)*. The category is sometimes stamped on the back of the paper, thus alerting you to the matching sequence to follow. But even if there is no such indication printed on the wallpaper, there is a simple way to distinguish at a glance between the two types: If the parts of the same design on the left and right edges of the paper are directly opposite each other, the pattern is a straight match; all other patterns are drop matches.

Unroll a length of paper from the roll you started with and hold it against the wall alongside that first strip. Shift the paper up and down until the pattern matches along the adjacent edges of the two strips; there will almost always be a small element of the pattern along the edges of each strip to help you match two strips at a glance.

Allow 2 inches for trim both at the top and at the bottom of the second strip. However, before cutting the strip from the roll, repeat the matching operation with another roll to find out which of the two rolls will be left with the lesser amount of waste. Depending on the height of the wall and the length of the pattern, you may discover that much waste can be avoided by cutting the strips alternately from the two rolls.

Straight-match pattern. In this type of pattern, the design stretches across the full width of a strip so that when strips are properly matched the design repeats horizontally from strip to strip. Some designs—such as plaids—may consist of small patterns that repeat horizontally several times between both edges of a strip. In either case, adjacent strips will be identical.

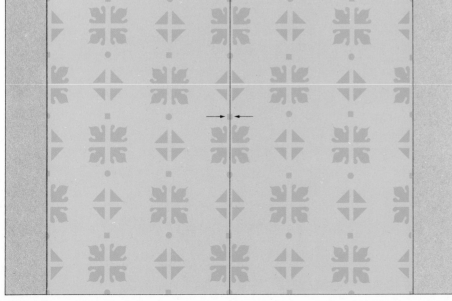

Drop-match pattern. This type of pattern is characterized by designs that extend beyond the width of a single strip. The most common variety *(left)* is drawn in such a way that the bottom half of the pattern on one strip fits exactly alongside the top half of the same pattern on the adjacent strip, and vice versa. This arrangement causes the design to repeat diagonally on the wall, hence the designation "drop match." Wallpaper designers usually incorporate a small element of the pattern along the edges of the paper *(arrows)* as a matching guide.

Joining Strips Together

All strips are hung and trimmed at top and bottom as demonstrated on page 96, but once the first strip is on the wall, all those that follow must be carefully joined together at their common seams. The joining procedure will vary depending on the type of wallcovering you are using and the section of the room you are papering—flat wall or corner, for example. Papering around corners is discussed on pages 100-101.

Because wallpapers are usually sold with their selvages trimmed off at the factory, the butted seam *(top, right),* in which edges just meet, has almost universally supplanted the bumpy-looking overlapped edges still found in older wallpaper. Only in special cases—such as turning corners or allowing for excessive shrinkage—will you need to resort to a lapped or a wire-edged seam, both of which are described at right.

A vinyl wallcovering—as opposed to a vinyl-coated paper—cannot be lapped because vinyl does not adhere to itself and the overlap would remain loose. When joining vinyl, you must almost always use the technique called "double-cutting," as explained on the bottom of the opposite page. There is, however, a vinyl-on-vinyl adhesive, carried by most wallpaper stores, that permits small overlaps when they are necessary.

Avoid stretching edges when you join strips of any kind of material and, except for very fragile coverings, use a seam roller to get a strong bond *(opposite page).* Because seam rolling works best after the adhesive has begun to dry, you will save time if you hang four or five strips before starting to roll the seams.

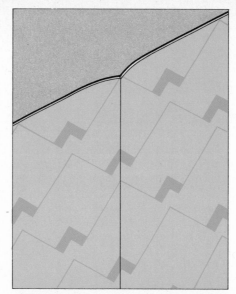

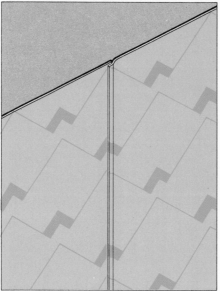

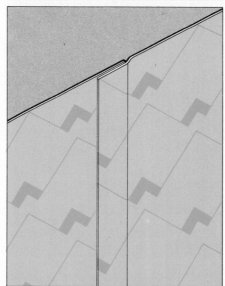

Three Types of Seams

Butted. Adjacent edges of two strips of wallpaper are brought firmly against each other until the edges buckle slightly, Because the paper shrinks somewhat as it dries, the buckling eventually flattens out against the wall. This is the best-looking seam and the one that is most frequently used in papering a flat expanse of wall.

Wire edge. In such a seam, the edge of one strip overlaps the adjacent edge by no more than 1/16 inch, hiding only a tiny portion of the pattern. This is the method that should be used if you have trouble butting your paper or if the paper shrinks so much the seams spread open.

Lapped. This type of seam, in which one strip overlaps the adjacent one by ¼ to ½ inch, was the most commonly used in earlier decades. It produces a noticeable ridge and is now used only in special cases—near corners, for example, where the alignment of the paper must be corrected because the walls are not perfectly vertical.

Making Seams

Positioning. Affix each new strip lightly on the wall, keeping it about ¼ inch away from the previous strip. Slide the new strip into position against the other strip. Keep your hands flat and well away from the edge of the strip to avoid stretching it. Move your hands about on the strip in order to get the pattern matched and the seam neatly butted. If you need a lapped seam, affix the strip about ¼ inch (¹⁄₁₆ inch for a wire-edge seam) over the previous one instead of away from it, and slide the new strip into place, using the same hand motions.

The roller method. When the adhesive is partly dry—10 to 15 minutes after you have hung a new strip—use a seam roller to press the edges of the seam firmly together and against the wall. Roll the cylinder against the seam with short up-and-down strokes until you have pressed the whole length of the seam. Do not use a seam roller on textured papers, flocks, foils or other fragile coverings, which would be marred by the rolling action; press the seam with a sponge instead (*far right*).

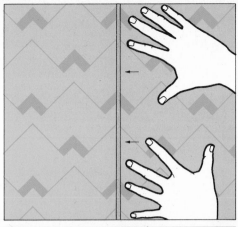

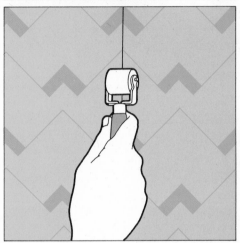

The sponge method. When hanging fragile papers, which a seam roller would damage, press the edges of each seam gently together with your fingers and a damp sponge. Manufacturers usually recommend using the same method also for prepasted wallpapers.

The Fine Art of Double-cutting

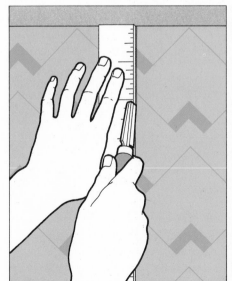

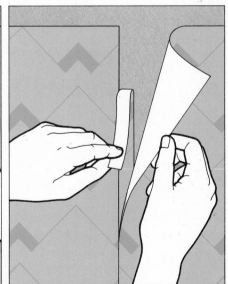

1 Cutting through the seam. Using a straight-edge to guide your trimming knife, slice through both thicknesses of the lapped seam approximately down the middle of the overlap. This will sever two narrow bands of paper, one clearly visible on the outside of the overlap and the other one hidden underneath.

2 Removing the outer band. Carefully peel off the outer band of the cut overlap. Use your trimming knife to deepen the cut if you find that the separation of the bands is not complete.

3 Removing the inner band. Now lift the edge of the strip from which you have just removed the outer band and peel off the band it covered (*drawing*). Press both edges of the cut together with a sponge. Finish with a seam roller, unless the paper is the kind that rolling would damage.

The Ins and Outs of Getting around Corners

Corners are slightly more difficult to handle than a flat wall. But you can achieve a professional-looking job by observing a few simple rules.

Keep in mind that the two walls that form a corner are seldom precisely vertical. In order to re-establish the correct alignment of the wallpaper strips, you will have to draw a new plumb line *(page 91)* on the wall immediately after you have turned the corner.

Also—and again because the walls are not truly vertical—you cannot bend more than a few inches of a strip around a corner without causing unsightly wrinkles. For this reason professionals prefer to slit the strip vertically into two sections to be hung separately, the first reaching just beyond the corner and the second lapping slightly over the first.

Slitting the strip also prevents a problem that would arise if you used a full strip when papering an inner corner: because most wall coverings shrink when they dry, the part of the strip that is pressed into the corner will eventually pull away; any pressure against the paper will then puncture it.

No such problems arise on an outer corner because drying merely tightens the strip against it. However, there is another hazard that must be avoided: if the lapped edge is placed less than ¼ inch or so from the corner, the edge will inevitably become frayed when people or furniture brush against it.

Note: The illustrations below and on the opposite page show the corners of rooms that are being papered from left to right; if you are papering your room from right to left, reverse the directions given in the instructions.

Inner Corners

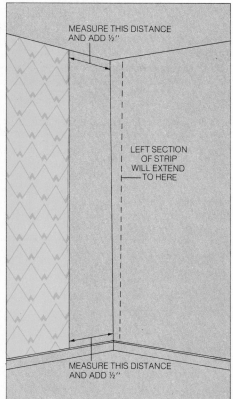

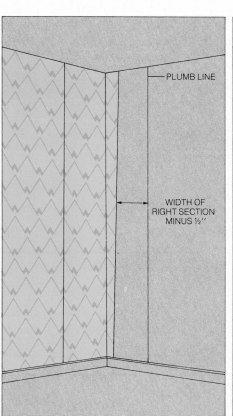

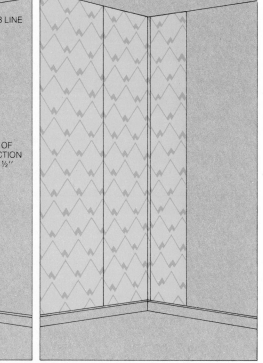

1 **Dividing the strip.** From the edge of the last strip that you have applied, measure the distance to the corner, then add ½ inch. Make this measurement both at the top and at the bottom of the wall *(drawing)*. Cut the next strip lengthwise, using the greater of these two measurements as the width of the left-hand section of the strip. Hang this section to the left of the corner and trim it at the top and bottom.

2 **Restoring the vertical alignment.** After hanging and trimming the left-hand section of the strip, measure the right-hand section and subtract ½ inch. Measure off that distance on the wall, as shown in the above drawing, and trace a plumb line through that measurement.

3 **Hanging the right-hand section.** Hang the right-hand section of the strip against the plumb line, overlapping the first section near the corner. In nearly all cases, the overlap will slant on the wall because the corner is not truly vertical (the drawings exaggerate the slant to clarify this point). The slight distortion of the pattern resulting from this slant is usually quite inconspicuous. Make sure that you double-cut the seam *(page 99)* if you are hanging a vinyl covering.

Outer Corners

1 Dividing the strip. From the edge of the last strip that you have applied, measure the distance to the corner of the wall, then add 1 inch to the measurement. Make this measurement both at the top and at the bottom of the wall (*drawing*). Then cut the next strip lengthwise, using the greater of these two measurements as the width of the left-hand section of the strip.

2 Turning the corner. To hang the left-hand section of the strip, smooth it on the wall as far as the corner, then slit the paper precisely as far as the ceiling line at the top, and precisely to the edge of the baseboard at the bottom. This will allow the paper to lie flat as you round the corner and smooth it on the other wall. Trim the strip at the top and at the bottom.

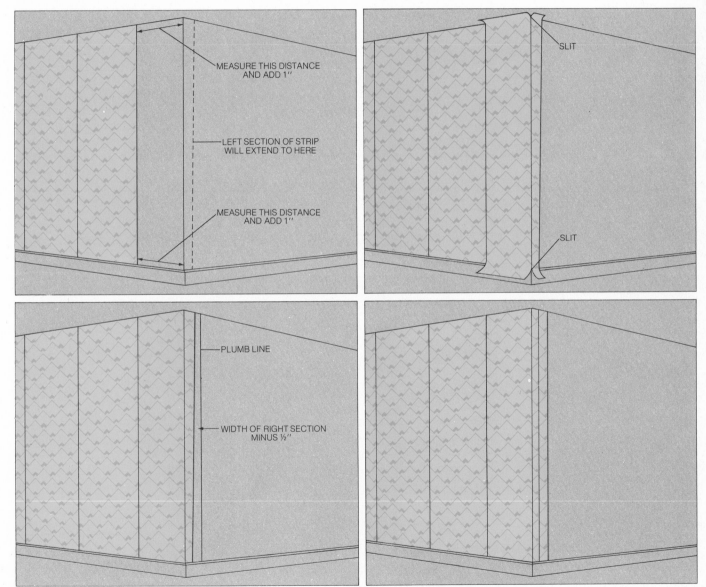

MEASURE THIS DISTANCE AND ADD 1"

LEFT SECTION OF STRIP WILL EXTEND TO HERE

MEASURE THIS DISTANCE AND ADD 1"

SLIT

SLIT

PLUMB LINE

WIDTH OF RIGHT SECTION MINUS ½"

3 Restoring the vertical alignment. After hanging and trimming the left-hand section of the strip, measure the width of the right-hand section and subtract ½ inch. Measure off that distance on the wall as shown in the drawing above, and trace a plumb line through that point.

4 Hanging the right-hand section. Follow the same procedure as for inner corners (*Step 3, left*). Double-cut the overlap if hanging vinyl (*page 99*).

Papering Doors and Windows

To paper around doors and windows that are framed by moldings, you must slit the paper and ease it around the corners of the moldings *(right and opposite)* before smoothing it on the wall. Casement windows, which do not have moldings, are treated more simply if you use any wall covering except the vinyl type: bring the wallpaper around all four edges of the casement and cover the inner sides, lapping seams as explained on page 104.

Vinyl coverings, which do not accept pasted lapped seams because vinyl does not adhere to itself, are trickier. Every lapped seam must be double-cut *(page 99)*, and the double-cuts must be away from the edges of the casement to keep the paper from fraying. Two methods, each designed for the least waste of wallpaper under specific circumstances, are described on pages 105-107.

To a certain extent, a room with casement windows may restrict your choice of pattern. Some pattern mismatches are unavoidable at the casements, and the best way to keep them inconspicuous is to use a small overall pattern.

Double-hung Windows

1 Approaching the window. Align the first strip that will reach the window as you would any previous strip, but smooth it onto the wall only as far as the window's vertical molding.

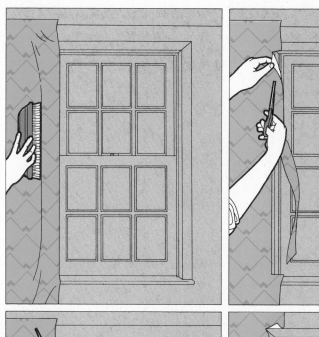

2 Removing the excess paper. With a pair of scissors, cut off part of the strip that overlaps the window molding, leaving about 2 inches of the overlap as a margin for final trimming.

3 Slitting the corners. Cut the paper diagonally at the top and bottom corners of the window molding, as shown in the drawing above. Each cut should end against the wall, precisely where the wall meets the outer corner of the molding. These cuts will permit the paper to be smoothed against the wall around the corners of the molding.

4 Smoothing the rest of the strip. Smooth the paper to the wall above and below the window, pressing the paper firmly against the molding.

5 Trimming the strip. With your trimming knife and a trimming guide to steady it, trim the excess paper along the molding, at the top, side and bottom (*drawing*). When rounding corners, especially at the sill, make a few cuts into the trim allowance to ease the tautness of the paper so it will lie flat. Trim at ceiling and baseboard as you did on previous strips (*page 96*).

6 Hanging the top and bottom strips. Hang as many short strips as needed above and below the window until the remaining distance to the opposite vertical edge of the window frame is less than the full width of a strip. Match the pattern as carefully as you would for full-length strips, and trim as usual at the ceiling, the upper and lower moldings and the baseboard.

7 Beginning to attach the last strip. The final long strip, which will be fitted around the two remaining corners of the molding and along its right vertical edge, must be attached first above the window. Match the pattern precisely alongside the edge of the last short strip and then smooth the long strip on the wall only as far down as the outer corner of the molding.

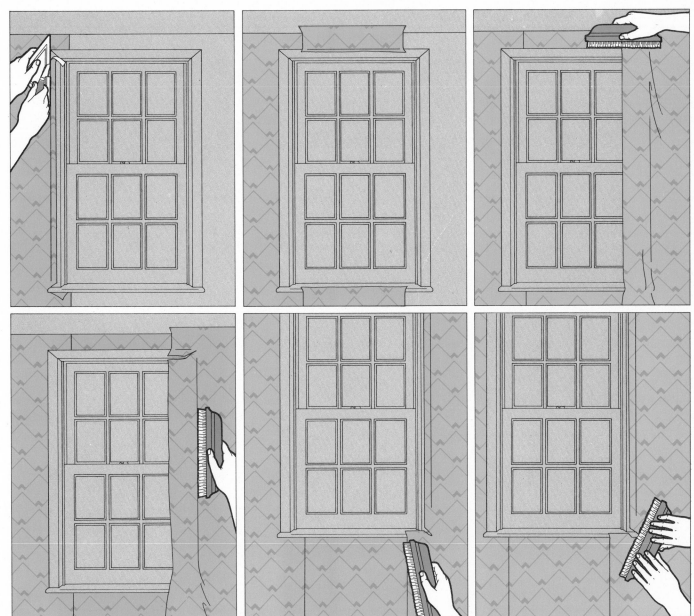

8 Papering down the second side. With scissors, make a horizontal slit in the paper about 2 inches below the top edge of the molding, stopping about 2 inches short of the vertical molding's outer edge. This cut relieves the pull of the still-unattached portion of the long strip. Then slit the strip diagonally at the upper corner as described in Step 3 (*opposite*). Attach the paper along the right side of the window molding, pressing just enough to hold it in place.

9 Matching the last seam. Cut off the excess paper and make a diagonal slit at the lower corner as in Steps 2 and 3 (*opposite*). Slide the lower left edge of the strip against the edge of the short strip and check the matching of the pattern along the seam. If necessary, lift the strip off the wall, around the bottom and along the side of the window molding, and ease it back into place until the last seam matches to your satisfaction.

10 Finishing the last strip. With firm strokes of your smoothing brush, smooth the entire strip on the wall, pressing its edges neatly against the molding. Finish the trimming around the side of the window, the ceiling, and along the baseboard.

Casement Windows:
Using Nonvinyl Wallpaper

1 **The first cut.** Hang strips of wallpaper in the usual way (here working from left to right). Upon reaching the window, hang the strip overlapping the casement—the recess around the window—as shown; be sure this strip is tightly hung. Trim off excess paper at ceiling and baseboard.

With a pair of scissors, make a horizontal cut in the strip, cutting midway between the top and the bottom of the casement. End the cut about 1 inch away from the left side of the casement.

2 **Vertical and diagonal cuts.** Working from the end of the horizontal cut, cut upward, then at a 45° diagonal to the upper corner of the casement. Make matching cuts downward from the horizontal cut to the lower corner of the casement.

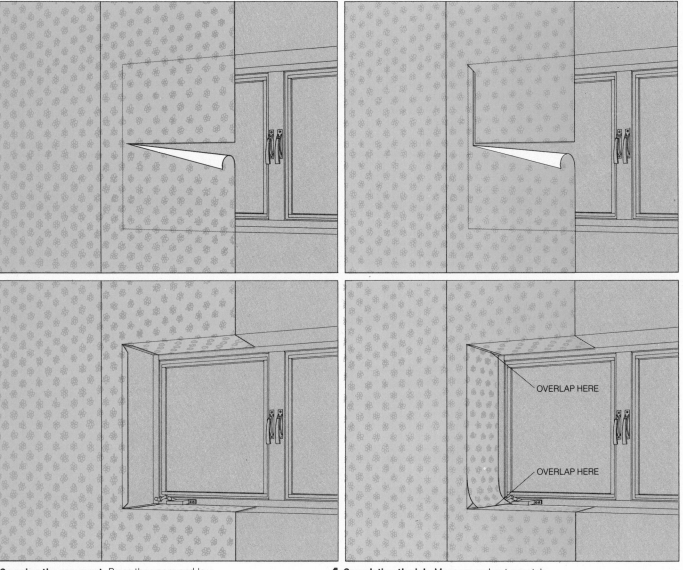

3 **Covering the casement.** Press the upper and lower flaps of wallpaper smoothly onto the top and bottom of the casement recess and trim the paper at the window frame. Press the narrow vertical flap onto the left edge of the casement.

4 **Completing the job.** Measure and cut a matching piece of wallpaper to cover the left side of the casement. The piece must be as wide as the side of the recess and long enough to overlap the flaps on the top and bottom. When you have hung this piece, continue hanging paper over the other side of the casement by the same method.

Casement Windows: Using Vinyl Wallpaper with a Long Overlap

1 **The first cut.** When a strip of vinyl wallpaper overlaps a large part of a casement window, hang the strip, trim it at the ceiling and baseboard, and cut away part of the middle section of the strip, using scissors and a trimming knife. Leave enough so that the paper above and below this section will completely cover the recess.

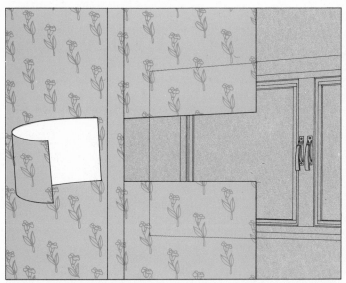

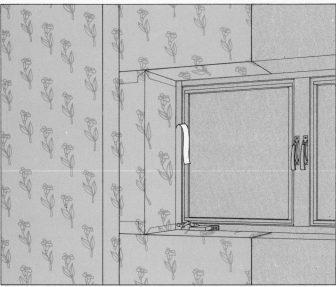

2 **Hanging the overlap.** Starting at the top and bottom corners of the casement, slit the vinyl on the wall with a trimming knife, making two cuts, each at a 45° angle and about 1 inch long. Then make two vertical cuts from the ends of these diagonals to the edges of the section you have removed; these four cuts are indicated by dash lines in the drawing below. From 1 inch below and above the ends of the diagonal cuts, make two horizontal cuts to the left edge of the strip (these cuts are indicated in the drawing by dotted lines) and pull off the two rectangles of paper marked A and B. Press and smooth the overlap flaps onto the top and bottom of the casement; trim these flaps at the window frame.

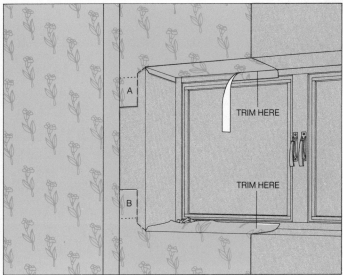

3 **Completing the job.** Measure and cut a piece of wallpaper, matching the paper you have already hung. It must be as long as the side of the casement and wide enough to reach from the last complete strip to the window frame, plus an allowance of 2 inches for trimming and double-cuts. Paste and hang this piece, and trim it at the window frame. Double-cut (*page 99*) the overlapping joints along the left, top and bottom edges of the piece. Follow the same procedure to cover the other side of the casement.

Casement Windows:
Using Vinyl Wallpaper with a Short Overlap

1 The first cuts. When a strip of vinyl wallpaper overlaps only a few inches of a casement window, hang the strip and trim it at the ceiling and the baseboard. Then, starting at the top and bottom corners of the casement, use a trimming knife to make two 45° diagonal cuts along the wall, each about 1 inch long, above and below the casement, as indicated by the dash lines at right. Make horizontal cuts from the ends of the diagonals to the edge of the strip.

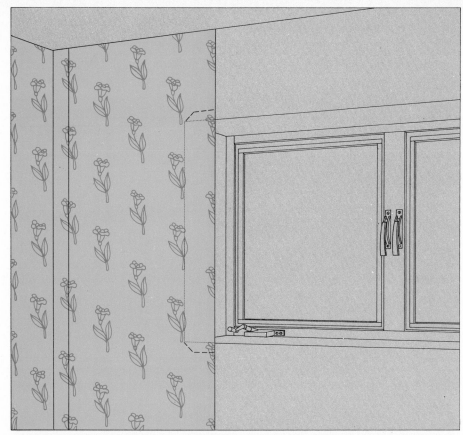

2 Hanging the flap. Press and smooth the flap onto the side of the casement; paste the projections at the ends of the flap to the top and bottom of the casement recess. Starting at the ends of the diagonal cuts, make vertical cuts to the ceiling and baseboard, and pull off the narrow lengths of paper above and below the casement.

3 **Fitting the matching piece.** Measure and cut a piece of wallpaper, matching the flap and of the same length but about 1 inch wider than the distance from the edge of the flap to the window frame. Paste and hang the matching piece flush to the window frame, then double-cut *(page 99)* along the overlapping joint between the flap and the matching piece.

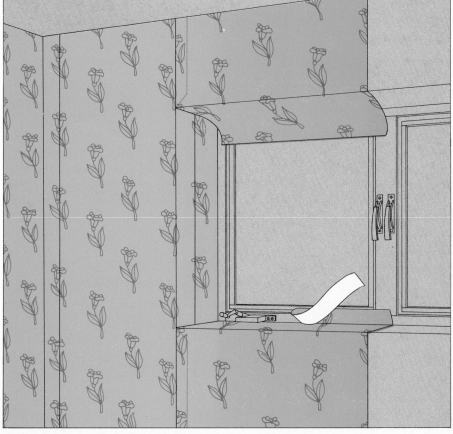

4 **Hanging the next strip.** From a new strip of wallpaper, cut a single matching section long enough to cover both the wall above the casement and the top of the casement recess itself, with an extra inch or two for trimming. Paste and hang it flush to the left edge of the casement, and trim it at the ceiling and the window frame. Cover the area from the bottom of the frame to the baseboard with another matching section. Double-cut all overlapping joints of the paper between the new strip, the previous strip and the matching piece. Hang strips by the same method to cover the rest of the casement.

Specialized Techniques for Working on a Ceiling

Not all ceilings should be papered. If a room is badly out of square you would probably be wise to paint instead: the complicated problems of aligning and piecing together strips of uneven width and length can cause more trouble than the job is worth. If you do decide to paper a ceiling, choose the pattern with special care. A figure with an obvious top and bottom can run up one wall and across the ceiling—but it will be upside down on the opposite wall. It is often best to choose completely different designs and colors for the walls and ceilings; this not only avoids problems of matching, but may also achieve other desirable effects. The apparent height of a low ceiling can be raised by covering it

with a light-colored paper and using a strong vertical pattern, such as a stripe, on the walls. To lower a high ceiling, use a horizontal pattern on the walls and a dark paper on the ceiling.

No matter what pattern you choose, you must take several preliminary steps. To find the amount of paper you will need, determine the area of the ceiling by measuring the baseboards (*page 87*). Prepare the surface thoroughly: it must be clean, smooth and sized (*page 84*). If the ceiling has a lighting fixture, remove or loosen it so that you can paper around it by the method shown on pages 116-117. And protect the floor from paste spillage with dropcloths or newspapers.

Once the job is under way, follow

these special guidelines for working on a ceiling: always paper the ceiling before the walls, work across the narrow width of a room—the strips will be shorter and more manageable—and, if possible, start the first strip at the short far wall opposite the main entrance. Work with a helper who supports the unhung paper, unfolds it as needed and checks the alignment while you apply the paper to the ceiling (from time to time, the roles of paperhanger and helper can be alternated). Above all, allow ample time for the job, and take frequent rest breaks —you will be balancing yourself on a narrow plank and simultaneously reaching over your head to handle a stubborn strip of soggy paper.

1 **Making the chalk line.** Measure the width of your wallpaper and subtract 1 inch as a trim allowance. Drive a tack into the ceiling about 1½ inches from the long wall and as far from the narrow wall as the width of the roll minus 1 inch. Drive another tack into the ceiling at a corresponding point near the opposite long wall. Rub a length of string with colored chalk and tie the string tautly between the tacks. At a point about halfway between the tacks pull the string down from the ceiling, then release it so it snaps onto the ceiling, leaving a distinct line (*dash line in drawing*).

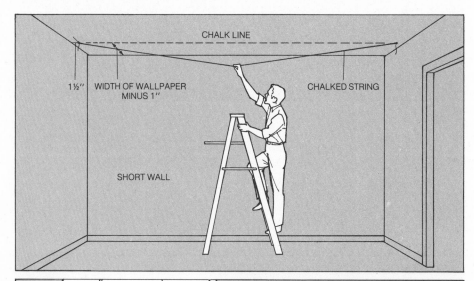

2 **Pasting and folding.** Measure and cut as many matching strips as you will need for the entire ceiling. In a rectangular room, each strip should extend the full width of the room, plus 4 inches as a trim allowance; if the room is irregular, with recessed alcoves or jutting sections, cut longer or shorter strips to cover these areas. Apply the correct adhesive (*pages 92-93*) to the first strip. Then, for easier handling while working overhead, fold the strip in an accordion fashion (*drawing*), rather than the customary double fold. Do not let the patterned side touch the pasted side as you fold, and be careful not to crease the paper.

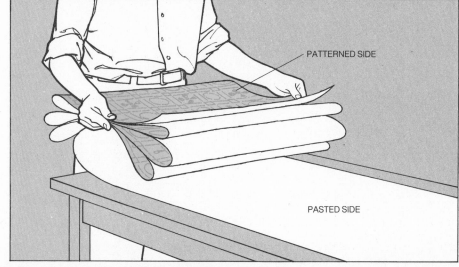

3 Aligning the strip. To reach the ceiling, erect a simple scaffold with two stepladders and a 2-by-10-inch plank. If the distance between the ladders is more than 6 feet, use two planks, one atop the other, for greater rigidity. With your helper holding the folded paper, begin to apply it to the ceiling at one of the long walls, allowing about 2 inches for trim at the long wall and 1 inch at the short one. Align the edge of the paper flush with the chalk line, first patting it gently into place with your hands, then brushing it lightly with short strokes of the smoothing brush (drawing). As you work your way across the room, your helper should open the paper fold by fold and check the alignment of the pasted section. When you have hung the entire strip, go over it once again with the smoothing brush, and make a final check for misalignments and wrinkles.

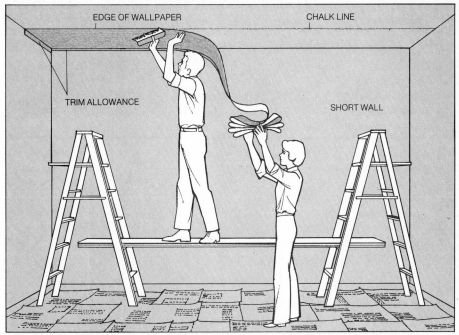

EDGE OF WALLPAPER   CHALK LINE

TRIM ALLOWANCE

SHORT WALL

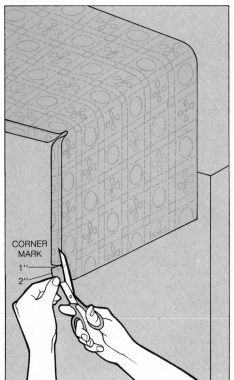

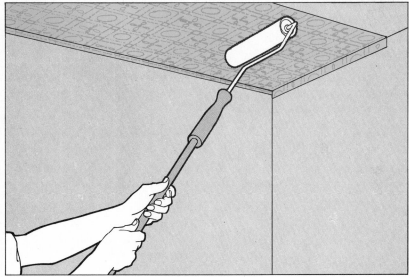

CORNER MARK

1"
2"

4 Making trim cuts at the corners. Push the paper gently into a corner with the bristles of the smoothing brush, and make a chalk mark on the paper to indicate the exact position of the corner. Slowly and carefully pull about 1 foot of paper away from the ceiling and, with a pair of scissors, cut a 1-inch-by-2-inch rectangle from the corner, as shown in the drawing. Realign the strip to the chalk line and smooth it back into the corner, using the bristles of the smoothing brush. Repeat this procedure at the other corners.

5 Smoothing and trimming. With a clean paint roller or a broom covered with a clean rag, smooth the strip firmly to eliminate any air bubbles and to bond the paper securely to the surface. Work first from the center of the strip left and right toward the edges, then finish the job with lengthwise strokes in one direction only.

Crease the strip firmly into the angles between the ceiling and the walls with the blunt side of a pair of scissors. If you are papering the ceiling alone, trim the paper at the line where the ceiling meets a wall, using one of the trimming methods shown on page 96. If you are papering the walls as well as the ceiling, trim nonvinyl papers to leave a ½-inch overlap; for vinyl paper, leave the full trim allowance to be double-cut (page 99) with the wall strips. After the first end strip is in place, hang the others in the same manner.

Handling the Heights of a Stairwell

Stairwells present a challenge to a paper-hanger's skills. The job can be both time consuming and exhausting. It involves moving and adjusting scaffolding often, climbing onto and off the scaffold platform again and again and handling extra-long, heavy strips of wallpaper. If the head wall of your stairwell is a partial wall, like the one shown on these pages, you will have to work with precisely measured strips; if you are papering a full wall, on a landing between two short flights of stairs, for example, you can hang full ceiling-to-baseboard strips. In either case, a helper is almost essential. If your stairwell has an extremely high ceiling, do not use the homemade scaffold shown here; instead, rent scaffolding and have it set up by a professional.

Prepare all surfaces thoroughly *(pages 84-86).* If you must paper the ceiling—extra difficult in a stairwell—do it before papering the walls. Estimate the amount of paper needed for the stairwell walls *(page 87),* and buy at least one extra roll to allow for trimming the slanting bottoms of the strips. A small, scattered pattern is better than a large bold design because slight mismatches will be less noticeable; precise matching is almost impossible with the cumbersome strips.

Measure and cut the strips for the well wall one by one to be sure that each is the correct length. With a few exceptions described on these pages the basic techniques of pasting, folding, smoothing and trimming are the same as the methods used for regular wall strips.

1 Hanging the top of the first strip. Hang vertical strips on the upper-landing wall by the usual methods. Hang the last strip as close as possible to the topmost stair; if the strip extends beyond the edge of the stair, trim part of the baseboard edge on the diagonal. Now set up a platform for the stairwell with a stepladder on the upper landing, a straight ladder against the head wall and a plank or planks between them *(pages 10-12).* Drop a new plumb line *(page 91)* if the upper landing is part of a long hall or forms a corner at the head of the stairs. Working from the platform, hang the top of the first well-wall strip. Butt the seam to the last upper-landing strip.

WELL WALL — HEAD WALL

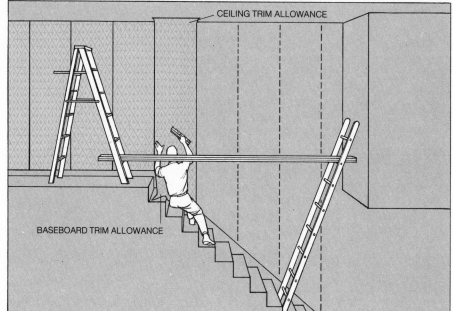

CEILING TRIM ALLOWANCE

BASEBOARD TRIM ALLOWANCE

2 Finishing the bottom of the strip. Climb down from the platform, move the platform slightly away from the well wall, and unfold and hang the bottom section of the first strip. (Trim away excess paper at the bottom left-hand edge of this and all other well-wall strips.) Move the platform back to the wall, and finish smoothing the top section. Crease and trim the paper at the ceiling line and roll the seam halfway down the strip, then dismount and repeat on the bottom section. Crease and trim the paper along the baseboard, cutting on the diagonal. Go over the entire strip with a clean paint roller on an extension handle or a broom covered with a clean rag to eliminate air bubbles. Hang the remaining well-wall strips *(dash lines)* by the same method until you have hung the last full-width strip before the corner between the well wall and the head wall.

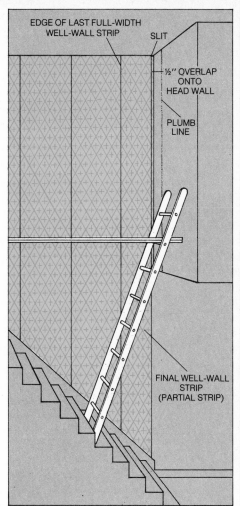

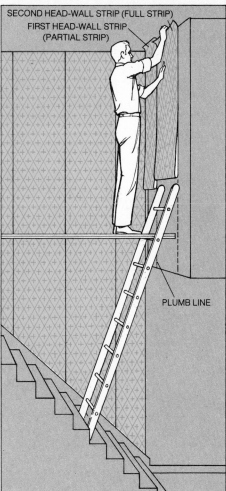

3 **Turning the inner corner.** Measure from the edge of the last strip to the head wall, add ½ inch. Cut a strip lengthwise, with the left-hand section measuring this distance.

Working from the platform, hang the top of this section, making a 1-inch slit at the top corner and smoothing the ½-inch overlap onto the head wall. Crease and trim the paper at the ceiling line and roll the seam, working down the wall as far as you can. To apply the middle of this long section, you may have to set up the platform arrangement shown in Step 5; if possible, work on the area from the staircase.

Continue applying and smoothing the section downward, and make a ½-inch slit at the point where the bottom of the head wall meets the well wall. Hang the paper below the slit, flush with the well wall, and trim it at the bottom. Measure the width of the right-hand section and subtract ½ inch. Standing on the platform, drop a plumb line at a point on the head wall that distance from the inner corner.

4 **Papering the top of the head wall.** For this step, it is almost essential to work with a helper to avoid constant mounting and dismounting from the platform, and to make sure that at least one—and preferably both—of the ladders are steadied. Measure the length and width of the head wall. To the length add top and bottom trim allowances; trim both the right-hand section of the corner strip and a second full-width strip to this total measurement. (If this wall is very wide, you may have to cut another full-width strip before you can hang the partial strip at the corner; usually, one strip will do.)

Add the widths of the strips, subtract ½ inch from the total, and subtract this figure from the width of the head wall. Using this amount plus an overlap as the width, cut a partial strip for the far corner. The overlap may vary: if the corner is an outer corner, as in the drawing, add 1 inch; if it is an inner corner add ½ inch.

Paste and fold all strips. Mount the platform and have a helper hand you the first partial strip. Hang the top only, aligning its right edge to the plumb line and overlapping at the corner; then hang the tops of the remaining strips.

5 **Completing the job.** Set the stepladder on the lower landing and rest the scaffolding so you can comfortably reach the bottom of the wall. Hang the bottoms of the head-wall strips, butting the seams. Smooth the overlap around the corner, slitting the paper at the bottom corner. When the strips are in place and free of wrinkles, smooth them with a clean paint roller on a long handle or a broom covered with a clean rag. Now trim the bottoms of the head-wall strips.

If you plan to paper the ceiling of the lower landing, trim the strips with a 1-inch overlap, and smooth the overlap for the outer corner onto the ceiling; otherwise, trim the strips flush to the bottom of the head wall. (Treat a molding at the bottom of the wall as though it were a baseboard.) Reassemble the two-ladder platform and trim the strips at the ceiling line, slitting the paper at the top corner. If your stairwell has three sides, or another inner corner, go on to paper the second well wall, then paper the remaining landing walls.

Covering Slanted Walls

In a dormer room, slanted walls and odd angles present special problems for the paperhanger, but the work is surprisingly easy if you choose the right pattern. Because some mismatches are inevitable, especially where angled walls meet, select a design with a small, overall motif such as random polka dots. Estimate the amount of wallpaper you will need by measuring the area of all surfaces to be covered as accurately as possible (page 87), then add at least an extra roll of paper to compensate for the odd-shaped sections you will cut.

Because of the difficulty of wallpapering high-peaked, sloping ceilings, many homeowners prefer to paint the ceiling, treating a wall that slants near the ceiling as part of the ceiling area. However, a wall that slants from floor to ceiling is generally considered part of the wall area. If you decide to paper the ceiling, hang the horizontal areas first (pages 108-109), treat slanted areas as part of the wall (Step 3), and finish by papering any remaining triangular areas (Step 5). Paper a recessed, walk-in dormer separately, rather than as part of the main room.

1 **Hanging the top of the corner.** Starting at the left end of a floor-to-ceiling vertical wall, drop a plumb line (page 91) and hang vertical strips (pages 92-99). Trim the strips (page 96) at the ceiling and the baseboard.

At the top of the full-width strip that overlaps the slanted corner, make a crease along the ceiling line as far as possible, then crease the paper into the corner diagonally. Trim horizontally at the ceiling line, then, leaving a ½-inch overlap for turning the corner between the slanted and vertical walls, cut the rest of the strip diagonally. Make a small slit in the paper where the ceiling meets the top of the corner so the paper will lie flat.

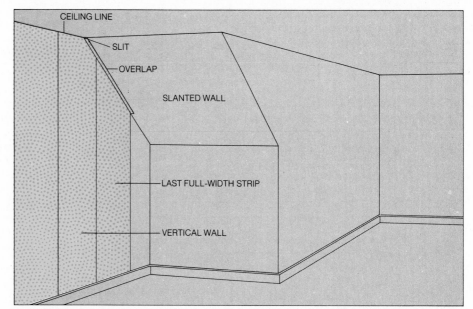

2 **Finishing the bottom of the corner.** Measure the horizontal distance from the edge of the last full-width strip to the corner of the short vertical wall —called a knee wall—and add ½ inch. Measure the vertical distance from the top right-hand edge of the strip to the baseboard, and add 4 inches. Cut a partial strip as wide as the first figure and as long as the second. Hang the strip, butting its left edge against the last full-width strip.

Crease and trim the top of the strip diagonally, leaving the ½-inch overlap for turning the corner. Make a slit at the angle between the slanted wall and the knee wall, and another slit at the baseboard. Trim the strip flush to the baseboard.

To mark the position for the first strip on the slanted and knee walls, measure the width of your wallpaper and subtract ½ inch. Drop a plumb line on the knee wall this distance from the corner. Using the same measurement, snap a chalk line (page 108) on the slanted wall.

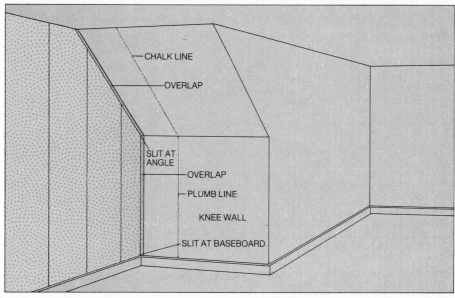

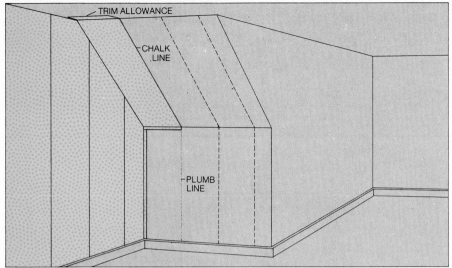

3 **Covering the slanted and knee walls.** Measure the distance between the ceiling line and the line where the slanted and knee walls meet, and add 2½ inches. Cut a full width of wallpaper to this length. Measure the height of the knee wall, and add 2 inches. Cut a second full width of paper to this length. Align and hang the edge of the first strip to the chalk line you have made on the slanted wall, with ½ inch of overlap onto the knee wall.

Align and hang the second strip to the plumb line of the knee wall, covering the ½-inch overlap. With the strips in place and smoothed, trim the allowances at the ceiling line and baseboard. Hang full widths of paper *(dash lines)* up to the last full-width strips before the outer corner, then go on to the next step.

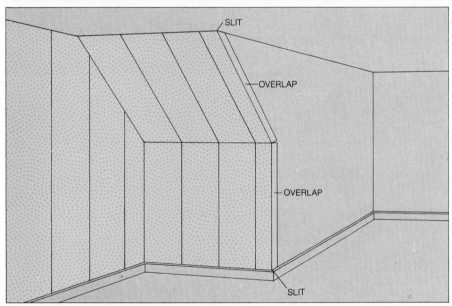

4 **Turning the outer corner.** Measure the distance from the edge of the last full-width strips to the outer corner, and add 1 inch. Use this figure for the width of partial strips for the slanted and knee walls, making them as long as the strips cut for Step 3. Cut and hang these strips separately, and slit the paper at ceiling and baseboard.

If the slanted and knee walls end at an inner corner establish the width of the partial strips by adding ½ inch to the distance between the last full-width strip and the corner. Then cut and hang the partial strips and slit the paper at the top and bottom. Measure the width of the unhung partial strips and subtract ½ inch. Drop a plumb line on the vertical wall this distance from the corner. Measure the length of the plumb line and add trim allowances, then cut a new partial strip to this total length and as wide as the unhung strips. Hang the strip, trimming the top diagonally as in Step 2. Using full widths, cut and hang the remaining vertical strips beyond the corner.

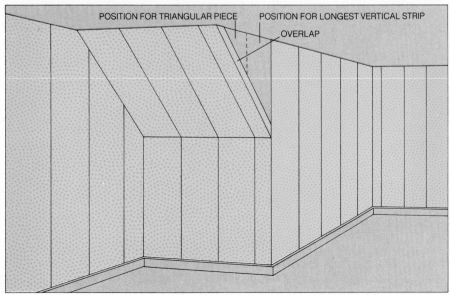

5 **Papering a triangular area.** Before tackling the triangular sections of a room, hang all the full vertical strips you can, allowing for overlaps each time you turn a corner, and dropping new plumb lines when necessary. Then follow the procedure below for any remaining triangular areas.

Measure and cut the longest vertical strip first, including trim allowances and using the full width of the paper if possible. Hang the strip, then trim it to fit—in this case, horizontally at the ceiling and diagonally at the slanted outer corner.

Measure the small triangle to the left of the last strip, then hang a piece of wallpaper cut to this size and shape, plus trim allowances. For overlaps, like the one shown here at the slanted outer corner, paste the seams of nonvinyl paper or double-cut them if you are using vinyl.

Allowing for Obstacles

The best way to paper around a fixture in a wall or ceiling is to paper under it—then the fixture will appear to rest against a surface design unbroken by any seam. To achieve this effect, you must remove the obstruction completely. For a receptacle cover or the switch plate shown on these pages, you need only detach a cover plate. For a wall sconce or the ceiling light on page 116, you must not only detach the fixture, but disconnect its wires.

If you prefer not to handle the wires and screws that form the connections of a light fixture, you can still achieve a reasonably neat job—only one short seam is needed—by papering carefully around the canopy *(page 117)*.

Never dismantle any electrical fixture without first removing the fuse or tripping the circuit breaker that controls current to it. This common-sense safety precaution is especially important in paperhanging: wet wallpaper adhesive can be an excellent conductor of electricity, creating a dangerous shock hazard.

Switch Plates

1 **Detaching the plate.** After you have turned off power to the switch, remove the two screws in the cover plate. Then remove the plate.

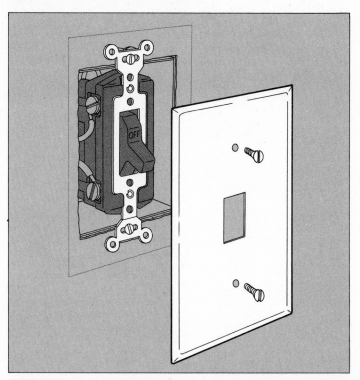

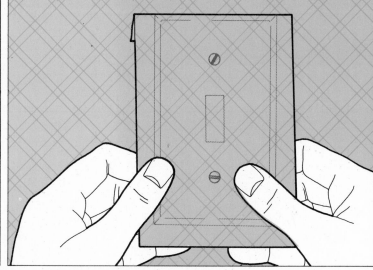

2 **Cutting a hole for the switch.** Paste and hang a strip of wallpaper in the usual manner, covering the recessed box. Split a small opening to uncover the toggle of the switch, and with a trimming knife or scissors, cut diagonally to each corner of the box. Enlarge the X cut into a rectangular hole, as big as the box, using the inside of the box as a guide. If you do not plan to paper the plate, screw it back on. To cover the plate with matching paper, follow the remaining steps.

3 **Matching paper for the cover plate.** With two or three turns of the mounting screws, mount the cover plate loosely on the wall. (If the screws are too short for working behind the plate, use longer screws or a pair of nails for this temporary mount.) Cut a piece of paper larger than the plate, fold the top over the plate and match the upper fold of the paper to the wall above.

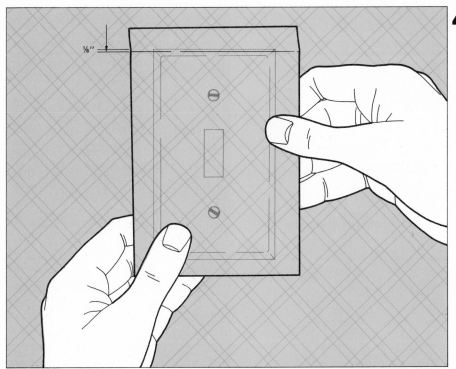

4 **Allowing for the bevels.** If the wallpaper has a small, intricate pattern that calls for close matching, you must allow for a slight increase in the size of the matching piece to cover the bulge created by the beveled shape of the plate. At this point in the job, the piece matches the paper on the wall perfectly at the top of the plate but poorly at the bottom. Move the paper about ⅛ inch downward (*arrow*), then fold the top and bottom of the piece over the plate and crease these folds firmly. The piece should closely match the wallpaper above and below the plate.

To match the side edges, follow the same procedure. Fold one side of the paper over the plate, match the pattern at this edge of the plate, then move the paper about ⅛ inch away from the edge. Fold the paper over the left and right edges of the plate and crease these folds firmly.

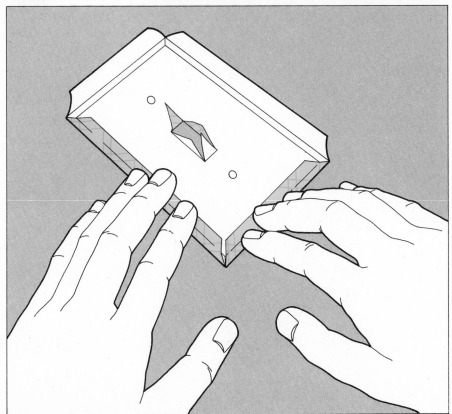

5 **Papering the plate.** Remove the plate from the wall. Apply paste to the matching piece of paper and mount it on the front of the plate, using the creases you have made as a guide for exact placement. Cut off the corners of the paper diagonally with a pair of scissors, then fold the paper over the back of the plate and press it firmly to both sides of the plate. Cut a small X over the toggle slot of the plate and fold the flaps through the slot to the back of the plate. Remount the plate.

Light Fixtures: The Best Way

1 Freeing the canopy. To hang a smooth, seamless strip of paper under a typical ceiling fixture, follow the procedure on this page. First, turn off current at the service panel. Holding the fixture securely with one hand, use your other hand to unscrew the fixture collar. When it comes off the nipple projecting from the recessed ceiling box, the canopy will drop, uncovering the box and wire connections. The fixture is now held only by fragile wires; support it carefully with your free hand.

2 Detaching the fixture. Still supporting the fixture with one hand, use the other to unscrew the wire nuts fastening the fixture wires to the house wires. Separate the wires, then lower the fixture carefully with both hands; the fixture wires will slide down and out through the bottom of the nipple. Do not unfasten the uninsulated ground wire that is attached to the ceiling box

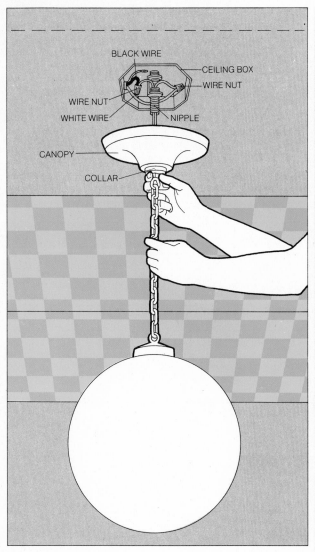

BLACK WIRE
CEILING BOX
WIRE NUT
WIRE NUT
WHITE WIRE
NIPPLE
CANOPY
COLLAR

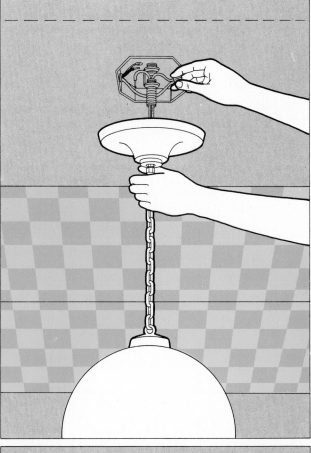

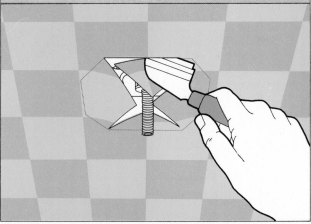

3 Hanging the wallpaper. Hang a strip of paper over the box, making an X-shaped cut with a trimming knife to allow the nipple to pass through. Smooth and trim the strip. Cut a hole over the nipple, using the inside of the box as a guide. Have a helper hold the fixture as you remount it: thread the fixture wires through the nipple, connect them with the wire nuts and refasten the collar.

Light Fixtures: A Good Alternative

1 **Hanging paper to the fixture.** The procedure on this page creates a seam across part of a strip, but eliminates the need to disconnect the fixture and its wires. Hang and smooth a strip as close as possible to the edge of the fixture canopy. Starting at the outer edge of the strip opposite the center of the canopy, make a cut to the approximate center of the canopy.

2 **Cutting around the canopy.** Working around the canopy in a half circle *(arrow)*, make wedge-shaped cuts in the paper, with the point of each wedge at about the center of the canopy and the thick end at the canopy edge. Then ease the strip completely around the fixture, working carefully to avoid tearing the paper. Make additional wedge-shaped cuts until the circle is complete.

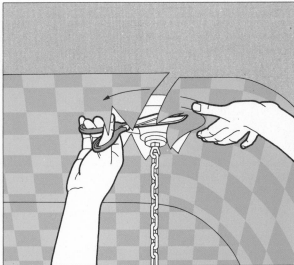

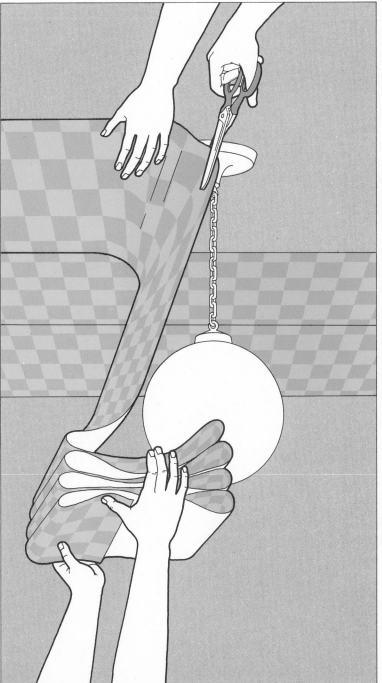

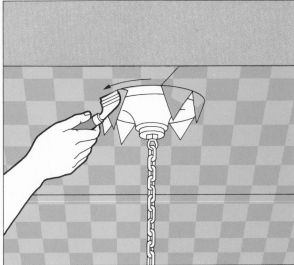

3 **Completing the job.** With a trimming knife, cut the wedges of paper as close to the canopy as possible. Smooth the short seam from the canopy to the outer edge of the strip. Hang and trim the rest of the strip in the usual manner.

Repairing Damaged Paper

Days—or even years—after your wallpapering job is finished, problems may appear. Fixing a loose seam is easy: paste it down again. The only trick to doing a neat job is to use a small, long-handled artist's brush to apply the paste so that you do not stretch the paper. Simple tears, when the flap of paper is still intact and not crumpled, also pose no special problems. Use the same kind of artist's brush to apply paste and, when you smooth down the paper, stroke it gently in one direction only—outward toward the edges of the tear.

Holes and bubbles in the wallpaper are more complicated to repair. Bubbles are generally caused by air trapped under the paper when it is applied. They may also appear hours or days later atop a spot that was not coated with adhesive.

If bubbles are near the ceiling or inconspicuously located, leave them alone. But if they are unsightly or in a place where an accidental puncture could result in a tear, use the methods shown on pages 120 and 121 to flatten them.

Holes have to be patched, and there are three ways to do that, depending on the kind of paper and the nature, size and location of the hole. If the damage is small or not noticeable, simply cut out a matching patch of wallpaper from a leftover roll or scrap and paste it directly over the damaged area. No one will notice it. (Use special vinyl-on-vinyl adhesive if you are patching vinyl or the patch will fall off.)

The second kind of patch is called a torn patch—one that is literally torn in a special way from a spare piece of matching paper. The purpose of tearing rather than cutting is to get a section with tapered, or feathered, edges so that the entire patch can lie smoothly in place with no white edges showing. This technique, which is described below, works best when the paper pattern is small and busy, the color is light and the hole itself is no larger than about an inch.

The double-cut method described on the opposite page will give you an almost invisible repair on larger holes, dark papers, and vinyls and foils, which cannot be torn. A very sharp, pointed utility knife is the best tool to use to cut these patches. The squared-off ends of an ordinary trimming knife might dig into the paper and tear it.

The Torn-Patch Method

1 Tearing a neat patch. Practice tearing on a scrap of the same or similar wallpaper before you make the patch you will actually use. Grasp one edge of the paper with the fingers of both hands placed so that the index finger of one hand is on the section that will be the patch and the thumb of the other hand is on the section that will be discarded. Rotate the hand holding the patch section gently upward (*drawing*) and twist it slightly in toward the other hand. At the same time, the other hand pulls down and toward the patch. If you manipulate the paper correctly, you will have a patch with an intact design on top and a feathered edge on the underside. The entire patch should be no more than 3 inches wide.

2 Applying the patch. If you use adhesive, apply a thin layer of paste to the patch with an artist's brush, stroking outward from the center to the feathered edge. If your paper is prepasted, wet the patch and shake off excess water. Handle the fragile edge carefully as you position the patch over the damaged paper and match the top of the patch to the pattern below. Make the final pattern alignment when the whole piece is in place. The match may not be exact but the discrepancy is rarely great enough to be noticeable.

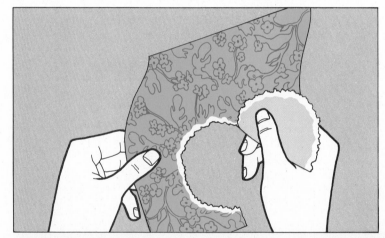

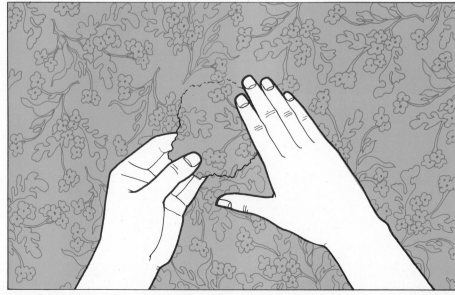

The Double-cut Method

1 **Before you cut.** Your patch should be large enough to overlap the damaged area by about 1 inch. The patch will be hard to handle if you make it smaller than 3 inches square. Whenever the design permits, have the patch fall within an enclosed pattern such as a rectangle or a square. Cuts are better concealed when they coincide with existing lines, so if the damage is located in one corner of a pattern square, for instance, as in the example at right, your patch should include the whole square anyway. Position the wallpaper scrap over the damaged area, align it to the pattern exactly and secure it with masking tape or with thumbtacks if the wallpaper surface might be marred when you remove the tape.

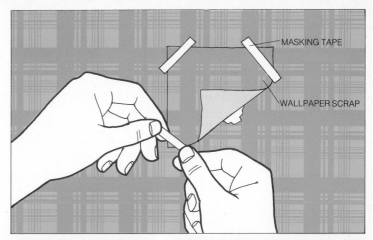

MASKING TAPE

WALLPAPER SCRAP

2 **Making the cut.** With one hand, hold a metal ruler against one side of the section you are cutting (*drawing*). Using a sharp knife, cut cleanly through both layers of paper all around the section. Try not to cut past the corners. Carefully remove the patch and the scrap it was cut from. If any part of the patch is still attached to the scrap, do not tear it out; instead, place the paper on a work surface and cut neatly with the knife.

3 **Making a space for the patch.** Use the knife to go over the cuts on the damaged section of wallpaper to make sure that the edges have been completely separated. Then, with the blade of your knife, pry up one corner of the cut area. With vinyls and most heavy papers, the whole patch should come out in one piece. If it does not, pry all around the edge, using a putty knife if necessary (*drawing*). Then scrape any glue or lumps of paper off the wall.

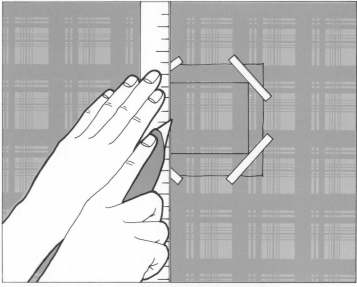

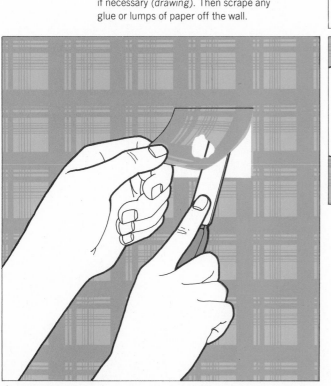

4 **Inserting the new patch.** If your paper is prepasted, wet the patch and shake off the excess water. If you use adhesive, apply it to the wall with a small artist's brush to avoid smearing any on the undamaged wallpaper. Hold the patch lightly with the fingers of both hands, taking care not to crease the paper. Insert the top edge into the cleaned-out section, pat it down lightly and then let the rest of the patch fall into place (*drawing*). Press it down lightly with a clean, damp sponge. After a few minutes press again with a clean sponge to be sure that the patch is firmly in place and that all corners and edges are down.

Cutting Flaps
to Flatten a Bubble

1 **Making the cuts.** Most bubbles can be eliminated by making two crosswise cuts, which let air escape and create flaps so that adhesive can be applied to the underside of the paper. Bubbles pop up in a variety of shapes, three of which are shown by shaded areas in the drawing, along with the best pattern of cuts to make for each shape. Slash along a pattern line wherever possible.

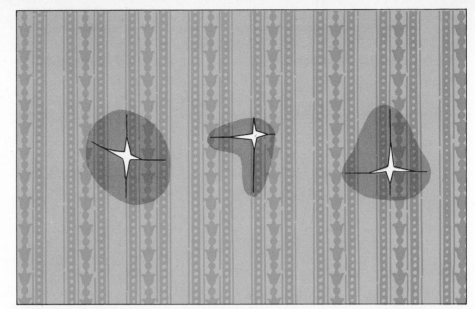

2 **Applying adhesive.** Moisten the patterned surface of the wallpaper flaps with a clean, damp sponge to make them flexible. Lift each flap in turn, taking special care not to bend it back far enough to crease it. Using a thin artist's brush, apply a small amount of adhesive to the wall underneath. If the paper is prepasted, wet the underside of the flaps with the brush.

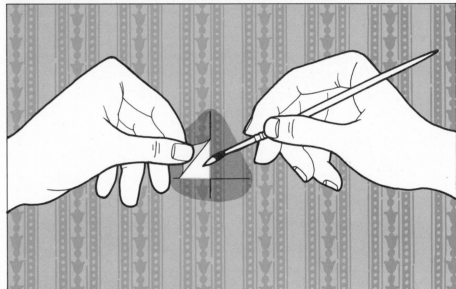

3 **Folding down the flaps.** Pat the flaps down gently in the sequence indicated, which evenly distributes any slack caused by stretching. Any overlap will disappear as the paper dries and shrinks. Sponge off excess adhesive after the flaps have been in place for a few minutes, but take care not to raise the flaps with the sponge.

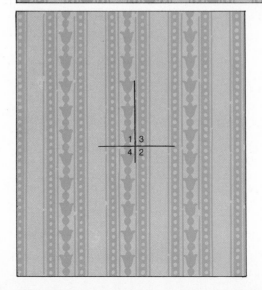

Curved Cuts
Instead of Straight

Cutting on a curve. On some wallpaper patterns, such as the one at left, a bubble can be flattened by making one curved cut instead of two intersecting slashes. The bubble *(shaded area)* in this paper has developed directly under a circular pattern design. When this or a similar situation occurs, make a single curved cut, three quarters of the way around the edge of the design and coinciding with the pattern *(dash line)*. Lift, without creasing, the curved flap that you have cut. Apply adhesive to the wall, using an artist's brush, let the flap drop back into place and press it down gently with a clean, damp sponge.

Cleaning and Maintaining Your Wallpaper

Most of today's wall coverings can be washed with mild soap and water. This is one job that, surprising though it may seem, is easier if you start at the bottom of a wall and work upward: if you work from the top, the dirty water flows down onto the dirt-clogged paper and leaves streaks that are very hard to remove. When you work from the bottom up, you can easily rinse off any water that runs down onto the clean section. Never use abrasive powdered cleansers on wallpaper, even on vinyls, and never use household woodwork cleaners that contain kerosene or other petroleum distillates. When the dirt is off, rinse the paper with clean water.

The material called cleaning dough, which works like a big eraser, can be used on nonwashable surfaces. Stubborn spots that do not come off with cleaning dough can be removed with a spray-can cleaner, or apply a paste made from carbon tetrachloride and cornstarch or fuller's earth. When the paste dries, brush it away. Whatever method you choose, test first on an inconspicuous spot because these cleaners change the paper's appearance.

Clear protective-spray coatings make nonwashable paper washable and add special protection over patched areas, which are more likely to hold dirt because of the cut or torn edges. Always use these coatings as soon as the adhesive is dry under the paper; otherwise dust may build up and be covered.

For minor repairs in the future, save unused powdered adhesive and wallpaper scraps. Keep the adhesive in a cool, dry place, making sure to label the container. Wrap leftover scraps in a sheet of brown wrapping paper and seal the ends. Store in cardboard mailing tubes to avoid crushing the paper.

When and How to Use Lining Paper

Lining paper—also called blank stock or backing paper—is an inexpensive, unpatterned paper used as a final preparation of a wall for covering. It speeds drying of adhesive after the final wall covering is hung, and it provides an exceptionally smooth surface on which to hang it.

Grass cloth, for example, tends to separate from its paper backing when wet; lining paper quickly absorbs moisture from the backing and solves the problem. Foils laminated to paper present the same problem—and in addition, foils emphasize every surface defect because they reflect light readily. A coat of lining paper can also be useful when one wall covering is laid over another. If you plan to cover a dark pattern with a lightweight covering, lining paper will prevent the old pattern from showing through the new. This method should be used only if the old paper cannot be removed.

Lining paper is hung like other wall coverings, but with simplifications (right) made possible by its lack of patterns and because it requires no trimming. Use the same adhesive for lining paper that you use for the final covering to ensure the best bond between the two.

1 Full strips. Start hanging lining paper at a door (drawing) or a corner. A plumb line is unnecessary. Cut a length of paper ¼ inch shorter than the distance from the ceiling to the baseboard and hang it about ⅛ inch away from the doorjamb, the ceiling and the baseboard. These gaps allow for direct bond between final paper and wall. Continue hanging all the full-length strips that will fit on the wall area you are lining, with ⅛-inch spaces between strips and away from ceiling, baseboard, and window or door moldings. Cut a strip lengthwise when turning a corner.

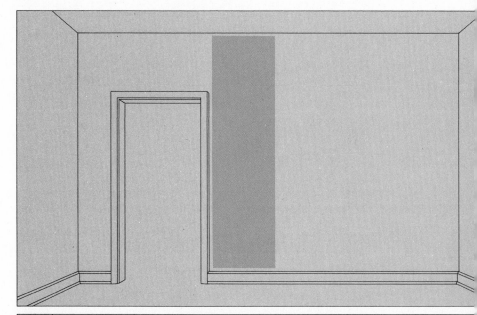

2 Short strips. In the areas above and below the windows, and above the doors, you will save time and paper by hanging horizontal strips that are cut to fit the space. Again leave ⅛-inch spaces between these short strips and the surrounding long strips, ceiling and window and door moldings.

Creating a Mural with Paper

Murals are wall-sized pictures that are reproduced on a number of wall-covering strips for a special decorative effect, particularly in a living room—although some are designed to be small enough for a foyer. They are available in all the principal wall-covering materials—paper, vinyl and foil—and some are laminated to a fabric backing for greater durability. They are sold in sets of strips 10 to 12 feet long, rather than in rolls. Each set of strips usually includes a few unpatterned ones in the background color to add to the ends, and additional blanks can be ordered if they are needed to reach the corners of a wall. The remaining walls in the room can be painted, but dealers also stock rolls of "companion papers" in harmonizing colors for customers who want to paper the rest of the room.

There is a large selection of mural designs, many of which have features intended to solve problems of space. Although the picture area may vary from 7 to 16 feet in width, the mural is often designed to fit a smaller wall by leaving out one or more strips (page 124), or to fit a larger wall by repeating some strips.

Before buying a mural, make a sketch of the wall, showing height and width. And, if you plan to cover the rest of the room with a companion paper, or to run a mural around a corner, sketch the other walls as well, including the location and size of windows and doors. Take this sketch to your dealer; he will then be able to show you the designs that are appropriate for your space and to tell you how many extra blank strips and how much companion paper—if any—you should order.

For the best appearance, murals should be hung on a very smooth wall. Remove all existing paper and prepare the surface by the methods described on pages 84-86; then do any necessary painting of doors and windows. Finish your surface preparations with a layer of lining paper (opposite page) to smooth all remaining irregularities.

A mural is hung like any other wallpaper (pages 92-99), except for a few special steps in positioning it, determining the sequence in which strips should be hung, and ending at corners (below and following pages).

1 **Choosing the height of the design.** The strips of a mural have enough unpatterned paper at top and bottom to permit you to adjust the vertical position of the design. You will need a helper to assist you. Have him hold the strip that includes the highest part of the design against the wall, and move it up and down until its position pleases you. Make light pencil marks at the left and right edges of this strip where the edges meet the baseboard; have your helper make similar marks at the ceiling.

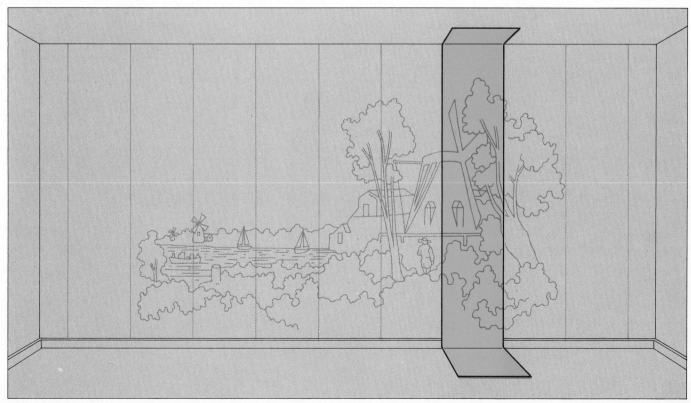

2 Marking the other strips. Lay the top of the strip you have just marked on a flat surface and place an adjacent strip alongside it, carefully matching the mural design. Transfer ceiling marks to this second strip *(right);* move the two strips upward to make aligning baseboard marks in the same manner. Repeat this procedure until all the strips have been marked. Cut off excess paper, leaving a 2-inch allowance above the ceiling marks and below the baseboard marks.

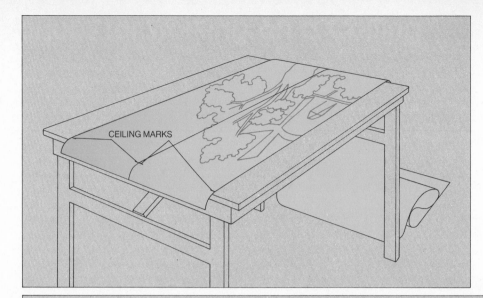

3 Hanging sequence. Manufacturers' instructions generally recommend the order in which strips should be hung, identifying each strip by a number printed on it. A typical sequence is shown in full at top right. This mural is designed so that one strip—Number 5—can be eliminated to fit the picture into a narrow wall. For the narrower version, the paperhanger would follow the sequence at right, below (the numerals in parentheses indicate the original numbering of the strips).

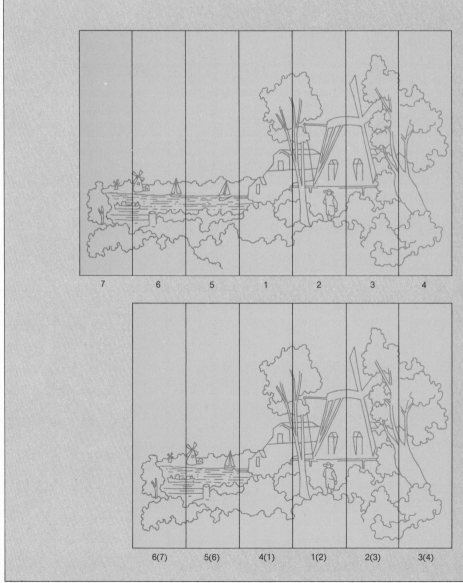

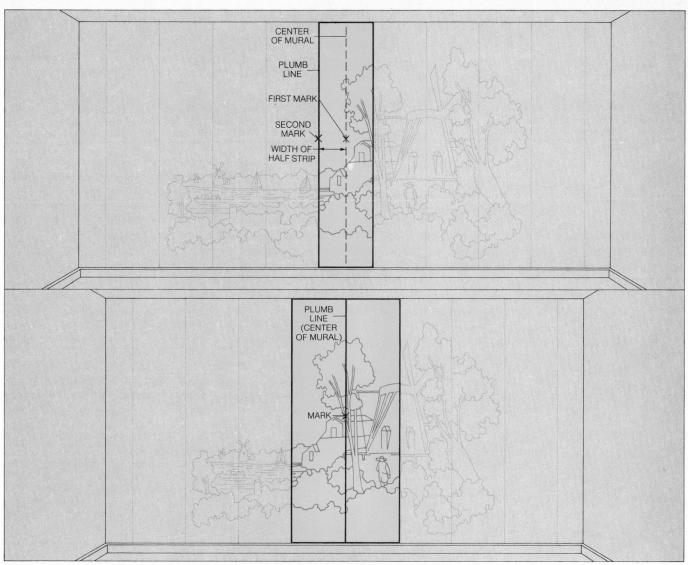

4 **Locating the plumb line.** To center an odd number of strips, as in the mural at top, make a pencil mark at the point on the wall where you plan to center the mural. Make a second mark to the left at a distance equal to one half the width of a strip. Draw a plumb line *(page 91)* through this second mark. The center strip will be hung at the right of the plumb line. To center an even number of strips as in the mural above, make a pencil mark at the point on the wall where you plan to center the mural. Draw a plumb line through the mark. The two center strips will be hung at the left and right of the plumb line.

5 **Finishing the corners.** If you are papering only the wall on which you are hanging the mural, trim the paper at the left and right corners by holding a straightedge against a corner and cutting off the excess paper with a trimming knife *(drawing)*. If you plan to continue the mural beyond a corner or to paper the entire room, follow the instructions on pages 100-101.

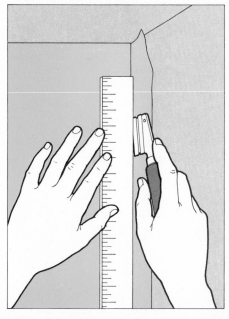

Picture Credits

The sources for the illustrations in this book are shown below.

Cover—Ken Kay. 6—Tom Yee. 10, 11, 12 —Drawings by Adolph E. Brotman. 13 —Drawings by Ray Skibinski. 18, 19—Photographs by Henry Groskinsky and Al Freni. 21 through 39—Drawings by Whitman Studio, Inc. 40 through 43—Drawings by Vantage Art, Inc. 44 through 49 —Drawings by Ray Skibinski. 50—Enrico Ferorelli. 54, 55—Photographs by Henry Groskinsky and Al Freni. 56 through 59 —Enrico Ferorelli. 61 through 69—Drawings by Whitman Studio, Inc. 70, 71 —Drawing by Nick Fasciano. 72 through 75—Drawings by Vantage Art, Inc. 76 —Tom Yee. 82, 83—Photographs by Henry Groskinsky and Al Freni. 85, 86, 87—Drawings by Whitman Studio, Inc. 88 through 107—Drawings by Nick Fasciano. 108 through 111—Drawings by Adolph E. Brotman. 112, 113—Drawings by Peter McGinn. 114 through 117—Drawings by Nick Fasciano. 118 through 121—Drawings by Ray Skibinski. 122 through 125 —Drawings by Peter McGinn.

Acknowledgments

The index/glossary for this book was prepared by Mel Ingber. The editors also wish to thank the following individuals: John E. Lynch, Technical Director, Technical Division, John J. Oberly, Chief Chemist, Technical Division, Edwin C. Price, Manager of Publications and Market Services, Benjamin Moore & Co., Montvale, N.J.; Gene Boals, Wooster Brush Co., Wooster, Ohio; Paul E. Davin, District Manager, PDC Division, Graco Inc., West Caldwell, N.J.; Constance Hacker, Thibaut Wallcoverings, Inc., New York City; Richard V. Hare, New York City; Mike Jennings, Henigson's Lumber Co., Larchmont, N.Y.; Lis King, Mahwah, N.J.; Alan Kline, Vice President, Lynn Ladder and Scaffolding Company, Inc., Lynn, Mass.; Mr. & Mrs. Alex Little, Old Greenwich, Conn.; T. D. MacQueen, The Gypsum Association, Evanston, Illinois; Royle Brown, Director of Technical Services, Ray Connor, Assistant Director of Technical Services, David L. Morehead, Manager, Editorial Services, Communications Division, National Paint and Coatings Association, Washington, D.C.; Clare E. Doran, Public Relations Dept., Edward Schenk, Architectural Representative, PPG Industries, Inc., Pittsburgh, Pa.; Diane Hood, Bob Paine, Richard Wens, Red Devil Inc., Union, N.J.; A. Rosenberg & Sons, New York City; Dr. Harold Schonhorn, Supervisor of Surface Chemistry Research Group, Organic Research and Development, Bell Laboratories, Murray Hill, N.J.; William J. Jones, Clayton H. Lange, Manager, Public Relations, Stanley Waller, Applicator Division-Specialty Products, Sherwin-Williams, Cleveland, Ohio; Silvo Hardware Co., Philadelphia, Pa.; C. Ray Smith, Interiors, New York City; Harold Swanson, Baker Brush Company, Inc., New York City; Massimo Vignelli, New York City; Stephen L. Wolf, President, S. Wolf Sons, New York City; Richard Ziff, 3M Company, New York City.

Index/Glossary